SPEED READING

Comprehensive Beginners Guide to Learn the Simple and Effective Methods of Speed Reading

TABLE OF CONTENTS

An Introduction to Speed Reading

Reading is an important part of our lives. Whether you have read articles, books, magazines, or any other text for school, work, or even pleasure, it's a skill we have learned when we were young. And the great thing about reading is that it helps us learn new things and expand our knowledge. So, imagine how much more you can learn if you are able to read at a faster rate while still being able to understand what you have read?

This skill is known as speed reading. This is a skill for people who want to optimize their lives and keep making themselves better. Speed reading allows you to learn at a faster rate, which also means that you will learn more in a shorter amount of time. It's one of the skills learned by those who are always on the path to self-improvement.

Once you have mastered speed reading, learning may come a lot easier. Of course, learning how to speed read is a process in itself. Speed reading doesn't just mean getting through the text with the quickest possible time, you also have to understand what you have read and recall all of the most important parts. In this book, you will learn all about speed reading. From what it is, how it works, to how you can learn it and make it part of your skill set, there's a lot for us to cover! By the end of this book, you should have all the information you need to start learning and honing this skill to achieve mastery.

How Does Speed Reading Differ from Normal Reading?

The mere fact that speed reading has its own name sets it apart from the "normal" reading process. When you learn speed reading, you're improving the way you read, too. The fact is, what's considered as "normal reading" is actually quite inefficient. The standard method in which we were taught how to read isn't as efficient as speed reading. So, you can look at it as reading (speed reading) vs. slow-reading (normal reading).

As you learn speed reading and keep on practicing it, you would be systematically breaking all of your normal reading habits. For some, this can be quite a challenge since they have been taught how to read that way and have been reading that way all their lives! Challenging as it is, though, it's not an impossible task. Just like any other skill, you can learn how to speed read as long as you stick with it and keep practicing.

On average, people read around 200 words each minute with a 60% level of comprehension. For those who find reading pleasurable and who enjoy the material they're reading, they can go as fast as 400 words each minute with a 70-75% level of comprehension. Of course, these are just average values. If you test yourself, you may discover that you read at a speed that's either higher or lower than these values.

But after learning speed reading, you may be able to read at a faster rate without having to sacrifice your level of comprehension.

Why is it Important to Learn Speed Reading?

Nowadays, learning how to speed read has become a very important skill in which to gain proficiency. We currently live in the information age wherein there is so much we want and need to learn. So much that if you don't read in an efficient way, you might experience an information overload. Since speed reading is a more effective method of reading, as it also improves your comprehension and focus, you won't have any trouble going through all the reading materials you want.

When you go online, you will find a wealth of information about anything under the sun. There are countless numbers of websites and online platforms, and each of them is filled with information both useful and trivial. Although some say books are slowly going out of style, reading remains to be an essential survival tool for this modern age. This is why it's important to become a more efficient reader, which just happens to be one of the main goals of speed reading. With this skill, you will be able to filter out irrelevant information to prevent information overload. It will also help improve your memory and comprehension because it helps you process significant information in a better way.

Speed reading can make your life a lot easier since you can just skim through the materials you have to read and only focus on the most relevant information. Learning speed reading is important because it helps improve your reading skills which, in turn, helps you become a more effective reader. Through speed reading, you can also differentiate the useful and useless information faster.

The Everyday Usefulness of Speed Reading

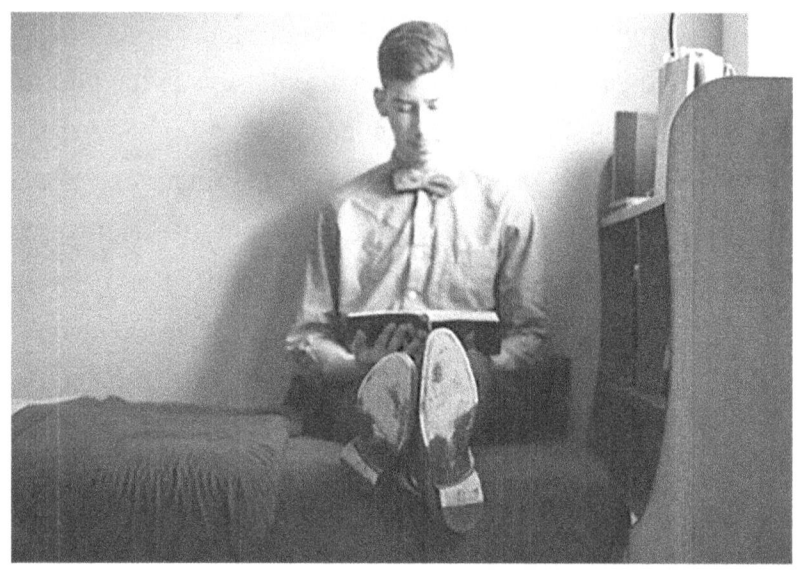

Speed reading has specific principles which can help you significantly improve your ability to process information and "separate the nuggets from the noise."[1] After some time, when you have already given your reading speed a much-needed boost, you will notice that you can easily breeze through newspapers, lengthy emails, magazines, study materials, and more. And you finally have the time to enjoy those novels which you had set aside due to the lack of time.

Of course, if you're reading novels and other material which require a more immersive reading, you can adjust your pace and read at a slower rate. But when you have finally mastered the skill of speed reading, it

---

[1] "separate the nuggets from the noise." Retrieved from https://www.myreadspeed.com/articles/

will become easier for you to adjust your reading pace as needed. This will be very helpful in your everyday life. So now, let's learn all about speed reading so you can start on your journey of understanding this new and oh-so-essential skill.

Chapter 1

What is Speed Reading?

- Speed reading, which is also called rapid reading, is a process which allows you to read books, articles, and other texts at a faster rate. This is a great skill to have, especially in our modern world where there is so much to learn! There are different methods to use for speed reading which we will learn more about later on.

- On average, people who read at a "normal" rate have a 60% comprehension. For those who try speed reading without using the right methods, the process cuts down this figure significantly to only about 50%. This means that simply reading quickly actually compromises your comprehension level, which won't be very helpful for you in the long run. If you don't understand what you're reading, it will be very challenging for you to study or learn what you're supposed to.

- Fortunately, true speed reading also involves good comprehension. You won't just learn how to read faster, you'll also learn how to understand what you're learning better. Although some reading experts don't believe that speed reading is very efficient because it decreases your comprehension levels, a lot of speed-reading advocates beg to disagree. In fact, they believe that speed reading may even increase your memory and IQ. Probably the main reason why speed reading doesn't seem to work for a lot of people is that they don't acquire the skill through the proper methods.

- Before you can learn to speed read efficiently, you first have to break or unlearn some of your existing reading habits. This will help pave the way for you to read faster while maintaining high levels of comprehension. This is the true definition of speed reading. And this is what you should aim for if you really want to become a speed-reading master.

The Truth About Speed Reading

- For a long time now, speed reading has been one of those skills experts have pushed on the general public. More recently, several apps have emerged which claim that they can help you speed read in an instant. Unfortunately, these "experts" and apps don't really bring everything that they advertise. So, does that mean that speed reading is nothing but a myth? Of course not! It's a real skill which you can learn given the proper information and practice.

Most people can read text at a rate of 200 to 400 words each minute. The best speed readers claim that they're able to read as fast as 1,000 to 1,700 words each minute! That's a lot compared to the average rate of normal readers. These claims aren't baseless. The experts are able to read text faster while still being able to understand and remember what they have read. To do this, they have employed some tried and tested speed-reading methods which we will discuss in detail later on.

These methods help you break the bad reading habits which you have learned in the past and have been using all your life. It may seem like an extreme and impossible task, but in reality, it's not. Let's take one of the most common examples to help you understand this concept better. Speed reading factors out the amount of time you spend thinking through unfamiliar and complex concepts which make reading a very mechanical process.

Normally, during this process, you would look at a word or group of words with what is known as "fixation." On average, it takes you around 0.25 seconds to look at these word/s before you move your eyes to the next word/s which, on average, would take about 0.1 seconds. After doing this one or two times, take a moment to understand the word or phrase you just read which, on average, takes around 0.3-0.5 seconds. All of these fixations and pauses add up, which is why people who read at a normal rate can only go as fast as 200 - 400 words each minute. But for speed readers, they are able to shorten the number of fixations and pauses which occur while they read.

This is just one example of how you can improve your reading speed as you unlearn the reading habits you have learned while growing up. Then, as you learn the other speed-reading methods, you start picking up new habits which will help you read faster. As you can see, speed reading is, indeed, possible. And it's an essential skill everyone must learn as soon as possible!

Why Should You Learn Speed Reading?

- We live in a fast-paced world where speed reading has become an essential skill. It will help you read larger quantities of information quickly while still processing it efficiently. This, in turn, will help you concentrate on the other tasks at hand. Here are some important reasons why you should learn speed reading:

- To improve your focus as well as your levels of reading comprehension.

- To enhance your ability to retain all of the information you read.

- To help you overcome any learning difficulties so that the learning process becomes easier for you.

- To significantly increase your reading speed.

- To understand how your eyes and your brain work hand-in-hand to process and retain all of the information you read.

- To increase your vocabulary.

- To save you a lot of time and to develop your confidence in reading.

- To be able to get through a lot more reading materials.

Although the mere thought of learning speed reading may sound intimidating to some, in reality, it isn't. Just like any other new skill that's worth learning, the more you learn about speed reading and the more you practice it, the easier it will get for you. As you keep practicing, your eyes will also thank you for it because they won't have to work as hard physically. The natural flow and rhythm of speed reading allow you to take in the information better. This is because you don't have to keep pausing to go back to what you've read just to understand it. This makes you lose your focus and, if the material you're reading doesn't interest you, it causes you to feel bored. Ultimately, you won't be able to retain the information you've read, no matter how many times you read the text.

Does Speed Reading Really Work?

When you have a lot of materials to go through and you feel like you don't have enough time to read everything, you probably wish that you already knew how to speed read. In such a case, most people look for life hacks and other time-saving techniques to help them overcome the challenges. There are plenty of speed-reading apps and courses out there, but will they really help you?

The fact is, most resources might not be able to help you reach your speed-reading goals. Especially those which claim that they can help you in record time and without much effort from you. Speed reading isn't a new concept. It has been around for some time now, and experts have been improving the methods to make it even more effective for those who want to learn.

Speed reading has come a long way since it was introduced. And, more recently, there have been technological advances which have helped out in a big way. Using different kinds of resources which offer help will go a long way. Later on, we will also go through some of the best apps that can assist you on your quest to speed read.

According to reading experts, the reading process consists of two major elements which are, absorbing the words and understanding or making sense of them. This is why you can only say that you're an efficient speed reader if you can read quickly while still understanding everything you've read. Otherwise, no matter how fast you can read words, the process would be meaningless.

Yes, speed reading works. But you can only become a master speed reader by learning the proper techniques and helping the process along. For instance, if you build your vocabulary and try to enhance your reading comprehension, these will help you out a lot to make you an even better speed reader. When it comes to speed reading, there's no instant fix. Don't think about it as a magic solution. Instead, think of it as a process, a skill you have to keep learning and practicing to achieve mastery. In fact, even if you have already become a great speed reader, you should still keep practicing and honing the skill so you don't lose it. You can also change your attitude towards thinking so you can find it more enjoyable even though you're reading "boring" materials.

Speed Reading vs Photo Reading

The only thing that speed reading and photo reading have in common is the term "reading." Speed reading began back in the 1940s through research and was later popularized by Evelyn Wood. Basically, speed reading is just like regular reading but faster. Rather than reading the text word by word, you read phrases, sentences, and paragraphs. And just like reading, speed reading is primarily a function of the left brain or the conscious mind.

On the other hand, photo reading is a more recent concept, as it came from research back in the 1970s and the 1980s. However, the concept of photo reading only appeared in books in the 20th century. Photo reading uses more of the right brain or the unconscious mind. Through this process, you learn how not to depend on the words written on the page but on the thoughts that go through your mind. Rather than moving your eyeballs quickly, you would make use of your brain more effectively.

Speed reading teaches you to read text quickly. Then, the better you become at speed reading, the more you will be able to pour through written materials while still understanding everything. As you learn, you need to consciously practice the skill to get better.

For photo reading, you should first go into a relaxed state known as an "accelerated learning state" in order to make you more aware. You have to allow your mind and body to relax so you become more receptive to all of the information written in the material. During photo reading, you can read books as fast as you're able to turn pages, as fast at 25,000 words each minute! Of course, during the first stages, you won't achieve high levels of comprehension because this comes later on when you reach the "activation" stage. But most people who start photo reading don't really worry about comprehension, so they never stress about the process.

So, basically, speed reading is a skill in which you learn how to read and comprehend text at a faster rate while photo reading focuses on more than just speed. Some people say that it's a new and different way to learn from written information. Of course, we're focused on speed reading on this book. So, if you want to learn more about photo reading, you can do your own research on the subject.

Speed Reading, Skimming, and Reading
Before we learn more about "normal reading" and all of its implications for speed reading, let's define it. Basically, reading isn't defined as a process of thinking about textual information so you can get the intended meaning of each sentence, phrase, and word. Remember that there are some types of literature which are intentionally created to have one level of ambiguity or another.

Reading is a process wherein you absorb the text then process it to understand what it means.

With the exception of those who want to leave their readers wondering what they just read, most authors want their readers to fully comprehend what they want to communicate. Also, they want their readers to understand all of the words within the text. Usually, the goal of someone who reads a book, an article, a manual, or other kinds of text is to learn new things. Therefore, successful reading means more than just recognizing the sequence of each word. You also have to understand the relationships between these words and make your own inferences about any unstated entities which are part of the described scenarios.

You can contrast reading with skimming since the goal of the latter is to simply move your eyes quickly throughout the text to locate a specific word, a piece of information, or to get the general idea of the content. As we will discuss later on, the rate of skimming can be as much as 4 times faster than the rates of people who read silently at a normal rate. Also, the levels of comprehension tend to be lower when you're just skimming the text compared to when you're reading it. This shows that there may be a trade-off between your speed and the accuracy of your comprehension.

So... where will speed reading fall when you consider the skimming-reading spectrum? The fact is, speed reading isn't really part of this spectrum. Instead, speed reading involves both reading and skimming. Through speed reading, you will read the content quickly while trying to understand it. One of the methods to employ when you're learning how to speed read is skimming. However, it will involve more than just briefly going through the text without trying to understand what it's saying. Speed reading is a unique skill wherein you will be able to use your speed and comprehension at the same time to achieve more.

Chapter 2

The Science of Reading

Bookworms all over the world can rejoice once they learn that there's an effective way to speed up the reading process. The same feeling may apply to people who cringe every time they are assigned a task which involves reading. For most people, they can read around 200 - 400 words each minute from the time they read the words, process the words in their brain phonetically and imagine what's happening in the plot (in the case when you're reading a novel).

But when you keep on practicing and you use proper speed-reading methods, you can learn how to read books and other materials twice, thrice, or even five times faster! Think about it, simply doubling your reading time could spell a huge difference in how you go through reading materials. The process of traditional reading makes you move your eyes from left to right, reading the words in sequence. While doing this though, your eyes tend to naturally search for one point in every word, and this could be the key to unlocking your speed-reading skill.

The point our eyes are always looking for in each word is known as the optimal recognition point or ORP. As soon as your eyes locate the ORP, your brain starts to process the word and its meaning within a matter of milliseconds. Then, as your eyes keep following each word in the sentences, you start making sense of them. Then, when your eyes find a punctuation mark, your brain will prompt itself to create a rational thought. Then your eyes move on to the next words and the next sentences until you've read the whole text. This means that the brain spends about 80% of its time trying to find the ORP while the other 20% of the time, it's comprehending the words. But when you're speed reading, you don't follow this same process.

All About the Reading Process

Before you can understand how you can dramatically increase your reading speed while still maintaining your comprehension, you should first understand how the reading process actually works. Basically, reading is a skill that has language as its basis, and it's not just a visual process. In most countries and societies, reading skills start at the age of 6. From that point on, it would take a child several years before he is considered as a "proficient" reader. When they first learn how to read, children have the tendency to read out loud. They do this to convert the printed text into a spoken form which is more familiar to them. As time goes by, they start learning how to read silently.

Printed or written text consists of marks and fine lines. Therefore, the perceived limitations of your vision are a significant restriction on your reading process. One of the most common methods of speed reading involves using your peripheral vision (again, we will discuss this in detail later on) to read bigger parts of the page and, in some cases, even the entire page rather than reading words one by one.

For normal readers who haven't learned how to use their peripheral vision to increase their reading speed, they use eye movements while they read. Visual acuity is higher in your fovea, which is the center of your vision, than in your parafovea or periphery, which is about 1°–5° away from the center of your vision.

The quick, ballistic movements of your eyes, which are known as "saccades," allow you to move your fovea to the words your brain wants to process with the utmost efficiency. Therefore, your oculomotor system, which controls your eye movements, also controls the timing and the sequence of your visual system's contact with the text. The decision on how long you fixate on each word and when you move your eyes to the next words is, to a large extent, controlled by your cognitive processes. This method of control ensures that each word goes into your foveal vision at the best possible time. This is how the reading process works for every normal reader out there. It's also the process which have to change if you want to become an efficient speed reader.

How Do Your Eyes Read?

Just like a camera, your eyes take photographs of the text you're reading. When your eyes stop at a specific word on the page, this is known as fixation. Most people read this way, and too many fixations are why they aren't able to read faster than normal. The normal reading process, which is quite slow, is similar to a camera taking photos of a blank space time and time again, which is just inefficient.

For more than a century now, researchers have studied our eye movements to find out more about the cognitive processes behind reading. The technological breakthroughs in recent years have made eye-tracking possible through high-speed video cameras which they connect to computers. Basically, this type of technology computes the eyes' location up to 1000 times per second, which allows the researchers to know which word and which part of the word the reader focuses on. This technology can show the fixation times as well as the saccades.

The results of the study serve as concrete proof of how our eyes move and how the reading process happens. For normal readers, both the fixations and the saccades occur at relatively the same rate. And these are responsible for the average speed that normal readers have, which is at 200 - 4oo words each minute.

But if you train your eyes to lessen your number of fixations, you will be able to read at a faster rate. Simply put, when you reduce your eye fixations, this helps to increase the speed at which you read. Rather than just focusing on one word per fixation, you can train yourself to read more. This is one of the simple changes which you can do to help yourself double or even triple your reading speed.

The Factors Which Affect Your Reading Speed

Whether you're an avid reader or not, there are certain factors which may affect your reading speed. It's also important to learn about these factors as part of learning how to become a speed reader. So, let's go through these important factors to understand them better and how they affect your reading speed:

- **Your level of education**

This is a no-brainer. Of course, if you have a higher degree, you have the tendency to read faster than those who have a lower degree. This is because you need to have superb reading skills in order to get that higher degree. Take, for instance, a person who goes to college. He needs to accomplish a lot of reading assignments throughout his college years. When you compare this person to someone who finished high school and stopped there, the one who went to college would definitely be able to read faster, especially if the material has a more technical or informational nature.

- **Your interest in the material you're reading**

Of course, the more interested you are in what you're reading, the faster you'll get through it. Think about it, if you were reading a novel with a very thrilling plot, you would rush through it just to know how it ends. But if you were assigned to read a book for work, which you find really boring, you might end up daydreaming or spacing out frequently, which definitely affects your reading speed. Not only that, but you might also have to keep going back to the parts you've already read just so you can understand them better.

- **How the text is presented in the material you're reading**

This is an interesting factor, but it actually makes a lot of sense when you think about it. It's a lot easier to read text which is printed plainly and clearly compared to text which is printed using a cursive font or handwriting. And the easier it is to read the text, the faster you will be able to get through it.

Some say that a person's age may also affect his reading speed. So, the older you get, the slower you might get at reading, too. Of course, this only applies to adults and not to children who are just learning how to read. But, even if you grow older, if you keep practicing your speed reading skills, then you may be able to maintain your speed and efficiency.

The Factors Which Affect Your Reading Performance

Apart from your reading speed, you also have to consider your reading performance. No matter how fast you read, if you aren't able to read well, there would be no point in speed. Just like the factors which affect your reading speed, there are also several factors which affect your reading performance, including:

- **Your phonemic awareness**

This refers to how well you're able to hear individual sounds and orally manipulate them to make words. This is an oral skill which you should have mastered while you were young. If you were able to achieve mastery in phonemic awareness, you would have grown up to be a fluent and proficient reader.

- **The alphabetic principle**

This includes how well you recognize letters, understand that words consist of separate letters, and connect the sounds with the letters when you read them on print. Basically, it refers to how well you're able to decipher the alphabetic code of words. The problem with the English language is that most of the letters have more than one sound, and a lot of the sounds have more than one possible letter. So, if you haven't mastered this yet, you need to do so first before you can even start your speed-reading journey.

- **Your fluency**

This refers to the speed and accuracy of your reading. If you're fluent enough, it means that you're able to read the text quickly and correctly. Gaining fluency involves a lot of practice. You can start with reading materials which you find enjoyable then move on to the ones which don't fall within your subjects of interest. If you're able to read different types of material with fluency, this will improve your reading performance.

- **Your vocabulary**

Having a good vocabulary means that you will be able to get the meaning of the words you're reading. Think about it, if you're reading an informative article or book which contains unfamiliar words, you won't be able to fully comprehend the meaning of the whole text. This is why it is better for you to keep reading, even the materials which you think are "boring," to expand your vocabulary which, in turn, can help you become a faster and better reader.

- **How well you understand what you're reading**

Finally, you should also have a good level of comprehension if you want to be a great reader. Part of this is having a good vocabulary but another part is being able to consciously and actively consider and analyze the meaning of what you're reading as you're reading it. Remember that comprehension is an important part of speed reading, so make sure that you never compromise this just for the speed.

Starting your Speed-Reading Journey

Now that you know a lot more about reading, you're ready to start your speed-reading journey. As stated earlier, this is a process and not a "quick-fix." Speed reading is a skill which you should learn and not something which you can pick up without putting in any work. Before we start, let's go through some important things you should keep in mind:

1. Speed reading is more about control and not just speed

One of the biggest misconceptions about speed reading is that people who are able to do this don't actually understand what they're reading; they just focus on how fast they read. This is just not true. Speed reading is more about controlling your reading speed, and it's not just about rushing through the text. You can look at it this way: if you're a car racer, your speed matters a lot. But what's more important is your ability to control your speed on the track as needed. This makes you a more efficient driver. In the same way, learning how to control your speed makes you a more efficient reader.

2. You must read actively if you want to become a speed reader

Speed reading requires you to become an active reader. This means that, as you read the text, you are actively seeking to understand it. To do this, you can prime yourself even before you start reading by asking yourself what you want to get out of the material you're about to read.

This gives you a goal which you will consciously try to reach as you are reading.

3. Know when you should slow down

Remember that a big part of speed reading is being able to control your speed. This is very important since you need to know when it's time to slow down so you can better absorb or immerse yourself in what you're reading. For instance, you may want to speed read when you need to get the general idea of an article and you're pressed for time. But you may want to slow down if you're reading a novel so you can enjoy it more. Basically, you should be able to determine how fast you should read the material and be able to control your speed to match it.

4. Never forget that speed reading involves a lot of practice

This is one thing that a lot of people tend to forget the moment they see an improvement in their reading speed. Yes, you will notice that you're becoming a faster reader, but it doesn't stop there. The process also involves being a better reader, not just a faster one. So, whether you're at the beginning of your learning journey or you've been on it for quite some time already, keep in mind that practice is key.

Chapter 3

Speed Reading and Comprehension

Right now, a lot of people are reading at what's known as the "normal reading rate." But, just like you, there are some people who would like to increase their reading speed while still being able to understand everything they've read. Simple as this skill may seem, speed reading can actually have a great effect on the different aspects of your life.

This is especially true for people who are considered "slow readers." For students, slow readers might find written tests too challenging, especially the ones which have a lot of instructions or word problems. In such tests, these students might not be able to finish on time. This, in turn, may result in poor grades, either in high school or in college.

The same thing goes for professionals who aren't very good at reading. If they need to learn a new skill through reading, they might not learn the skill as fast as the other employees. Also, slow readers have the tendency to acquire less information when they're reading websites, magazines, newspapers, and more, all because they don't have enough time to read the resources fully. Furthermore, slow readers may also experience difficulty with comprehension, even though they're already reading at a slower rate!

Generally, slow readers read at a rate of 200 words each minute or lower. Speed readers, on the other hand, can read as much as 600-700 words each minute or higher depending on the person's skill. If you've learned the skill of speed reading well, you will be able to read quickly without sacrificing your comprehension, which is also an important part of reading.

A lot of "very slow readers" tend to move their lips as they're reading; this is a kind of subvocalization. There's another type of subvocalization which occurs when a person says the words he's reading. By definition, subvocalization is a process where you read out loud, and this tends to slow down your reading since you have to pronounce each of the words one at a time. If you can train yourself to stop subvocalizing (which we will discuss in detail later on), you will be able to read at a much faster rate.

There are other ways you can employ to increase both your speed and your comprehension. But, to become a successful and efficient speed reader, you should use the proper methods. That way you can improve your reading skill without compromising your comprehension or any other skills.

Is It Possible to Speed Read with Comprehension?

Reading comprehension is a type of cognitive process which requires different strategies and skills. This is one of the most important parts of reading, which is why a lot of people want to learn how to improve their comprehension skills. We've already established that speed reading can (and must) involve comprehension too. For you to improve your comprehension skills, you should understand the factors which contribute to it.

- **Background knowledge**

This factor plays a huge role in your reading comprehension. When you're trying to understand a text, you need to depend on your background knowledge to connect the things you already know to what you're reading. Both your literary knowledge and real-world experiences are part of your background knowledge. So, having background knowledge may help improve your reading comprehension.

- **Vocabulary and fluency**

You may have noticed that these factors are also part of your reading performance. This is because your vocabulary and fluency are both essential in the process of reading. To understand what you're reading, having both these factors will go a long way. If you want to improve your vocabulary, you should be able to recognize the word's definition, part of speech, context clues, and how the word works in the sentence. On the other hand, you can also develop your fluency through practice. This will help you understand and remember what you've read with expression, accuracy, and at a faster rate.

- **Critical thinking**

Finally, another important part of comprehension is critical thinking. With this skill, you can actively respond to what you're reading more effectively. As you're reading, you will be able to find the main idea as well as the supporting details of the text. You will also be able to determine the overall structure of what you're reading, along with the sequence of the events.

Speed Reading and Comprehension

Speed reading and comprehension can go hand-in-hand, and when they do, it creates a winning combination. There's a significant difference between reading mechanically at an impressively high speed and reading at a high speed but with comprehension. There is a true difference between these two, and only one of them will allow you to improve.

Comprehension is a vital part of reading no matter what form it takes. Think about it, how often do you read something just for the sake of reading? Chances are, you don't do this a lot. You read to learn new things, to be informed of the current trends and events, for pleasure, and more. Written language always has been one of the most effective methods of communication, and the primary goal of speed reading is to allow you to absorb more information faster. In other words, you'll to be able to take in information quickly and more efficiently.

It's time to learn more about dynamic comprehension and visualization. These mean that, as you're reading, your mind forms visual pictures rather than repeating the words you've read in your mind or mentally "listening" to yourself. If you're able to achieve this, you'll find that it's incredibly effective. For instance, if you're reading a novel, it will seem to you like you're actually "inside" the story. Or if you're reading informational text, say, about some new technologies, your reading experience will allow you to visualize how these technological devices work.

The fact is, human beings are basically visual creatures. Our sights are a vital part of our learning processes. Language isn't one of the mind's natural tools. Instead, it's a tool that we learn. For you to understand what you're reading while you're speed reading, you should first "translate" the worded language into a language in your mind which just happens to be the process of visualization. If you're able to do this, you will find out that your reading comprehension can get a significant boost!

If you want to begin using this technique alongside your mechanical skill of speed reading, the best type of material to start with are fictional books and stories which you're very interested in, rather than factual manuals or reports. Such materials will make it easier for you to improve your visualization and comprehension skills. Then, when you feel more confident with these skills, then you may try moving on to applying them to technical or factual reading materials.

Some experts believe that speed reading is actually an essential part of dynamic comprehension and visualization. Speed reading is a skill which trains the mechanical part of your reading skills to become as efficient as possible. However, this same mechanical part of reading is the one which slows down your visualization skill. This is because the speed of visualization works as fast as the speed of the human mind, which is really fast! So, when you improve this mechanical part of reading to make it as fast as the human mind, you will be able to maximize your reading as well as your comprehension. You can easily increase your reading speed and still understand and remember everything you've read.

But in order to improve both your reading speed and your comprehension, you have a lot of work to do. We've talked about some "bad habits" you may have to unlearn while you are learning more efficient reading habits. This is probably one of the most challenging parts of your speed-reading journey because you've learned and used these habits all your life. But, if you're able to unlearn the things which are holding you back, you will be able to learn speed reading faster and more efficiently. In doing this and in practicing over and over, you'll see yourself improving more and more.

Some Helpful Tips

Whether you're a high school student, a college student or a professional, you may, at one time, feel overwhelmed with the mere thought of having to read large quantities of reading materials in a short amount of time without compromising your comprehension of those important materials. Some studies have suggested that, when speed reading is done properly, it can actually allow you to achieve higher levels of comprehension compared to the traditional techniques used for reading. Some of the best speed readers can go as fast as 1,000 words each minute, which is a huge improvement over the normal reading speed of 400 words each minute. To help you out, here are some helpful tips to keep in mind:

- **Improving your vocabulary**

We've already established the importance of vocabulary in reading performance and comprehension. You will only be able to fully comprehend the material you're speed reading if your vocabulary is adequate enough to be able to quickly understand and process the words you're reading.

This is an important step to take, especially if your studies or your work involve reading informational materials which include a lot of new terminologies and concepts which are potentially difficult. So, before you try improving your speed, you may first need to focus on improving your vocabulary. You can do this by reading different kinds of text (using your normal reading rate) while also trying to find out the meanings of the suffixes and prefixes which are commonly used in sentences. This will help you figure out the definitions of the words you're not familiar with. Also, have a thesaurus or a dictionary on hand so every time you're reading; it's easy for you to use the books as a reference for the words you don't understand.

- **Never forget the importance of practice**

This is a tip we will keep mentioning because it's one of the most important. Remember that speed reading is a skill, so you need to keep on honing it if you want it to improve. People who consistently endeavor to enhance their reading speed and comprehension skills through daily practice will notice a significant improvement in those skills, especially when you read different kinds of material such as novels, newspapers, magazines, research journals, and so on.

Different types of reading materials are effective for honing your speed-reading skills, so you're exposed to different terminologies and concepts. On the other hand, abstract types of reading materials, such as legal abstracts, poetry, and the like, aren't very effective because they convey more precise information and important details.

- **Learn the proper speed-reading methods**

There are different speed-reading methods that can help you on your journey to learning the new skill. If you want to become an effective speed reader or you want to master the skill, then you should learn all of these methods. This is the best way to learn how to speed read properly and effectively. In the next few chapters, we will discuss these methods one at a time. That way you will be better equipped when you start learning how to improve your reading speed, and you will enrich your life.

- **Take care of yourself and schedule your speed-reading learning sessions**

After you've made the decision to start learning how to speed read, you must commit to it. No matter how busy your schedule is, you should find time to practice your skill or at least learn another one of the speed-reading methods. Also, procrastination can be a very powerful thing. But if you give into it, months after you've started the learning process, you'll realize that you've skipped out on a lot of practice time, and you've already forgotten the first concepts you've learned.

Just like any other new skill, learning speed reading involves a lot of time and effort. But no matter how much you want to master the skill, you shouldn't compromise your health just to do this, either. Set aside time each day to hone your skills, but don't overdo it. Remember that you still have other things to do in your daily routine, and you don't have the luxury to spend each and every day doing nothing but speed reading. The best thing you can do is incorporate speed reading into your life. Make it a daily part of your life until it has become one of your habits. Eventually, you won't even feel like it's a chore. Instead, it will become just one thing you're used to doing.

These are some helpful tips to keep in mind if you're planning to learn how to speed read. This essential skill will truly help you out in a lot of ways, and it will be a huge part of your self-improvement. Still not convinced? In the next chapter, let's learn about the benefits of speed reading and how it will improve your life.

Chapter 4

The Benefits of Speed Reading

For some people, the thought of having to read a book, an article, or some other form of text is dreadful because it takes them forever just to get through one paragraph. Sadly, more and more people are starting to feel this way, especially in this quick-paced, modern world. Nowadays, a lot of people put off reading books and other printed materials just because they feel like going through them takes too much time.

The good news is, you don't always have to worry about how slow you read. You can improve your reading speed along with your comprehension so that you won't have to see reading as a chore. After learning the skill of speed reading, you might remember why you loved reading in the first place! You won't have to worry about "wasting" a lot of time just because you feel like you don't read fast enough. Learning how to speed read involves a lot of time and effort, but, as we've said, it's not an impossible task. Keep up with this task and you'll find out that you can actually read a lot faster than you ever imagined.

There are different reasons why people read at a slower rate. But one of the main reasons is because we were taught to read this way from the beginning. There are different methods and tools which can help you overcome this barrier. Once you've done that, you can start increasing your reading speed so you can finish a lot more reading materials than you could do in the past. And, if you do this properly, you will be able to comprehend and remember everything you've read, too. Those who have mastered the skill are even able to learn everything they need to without reading the entire article, book, or any other type of reading material!

How to Speed Read

Speed reading is a skill wherein you quickly identify and absorb phrases and sentences on a page of printed text all at the same time instead of reading the words one by one. We have to process more and more information each day, and it is increasing. Whether you need to read articles on websites, reports, memos, emails, and more for work, school or home, there's really a lot to absorb. Because of this, we may feel a lot of pressure in terms of having to get through all of this information faster so we can stay updated and use the information we've learned to make wise decisions.

Most people in the world right now are average readers. While some are speed readers, some are slow readers, and others are illiterate. Of course, there are some people who have a natural speed-reading skill. If you're one of these lucky people and you consciously try to learn speed reading, you can even double or triple your natural speed. Basically, all speed-reading methods share one similarity. You need to avoid pronouncing each of the words and "hearing" them in your mind as you're reading. This is a process known as "subvocalization," and it's one of the most common reasons why most people read inefficiently. Instead, you must learn how to "skim" through phrases or lines as your mind is able to comprehend words faster than you're able to say them.

One clever way to prevent yourself from subvocalizing is to concentrate on groups or blocks of words instead of concentrating on the individual words themselves. You can do this if you try to relax then expand or "soften" your gaze when you look at the page. That way, you won't see the words as separate. As you keep practicing this method, your eyes will learn how to quickly skip across the printed text. Then, as you're approaching the end of a sentence or a line of text, you will use your peripheral vision to see the last group of words. This helps prevent pauses or fixations which commonly occur with normal readers. That way, you are able to scan across and scan down to the next sentences at a faster rate. Here, we just described all of the most important speed-reading methods in summation. Later on, we will discuss these methods one at a time, so you can understand them better.

All of these speed-reading methods will help you learn how to speed read efficiently. Remember that effective and successful speed reading is a combination of speed and comprehension. A lot of skeptics believe that the faster you're able to read, the less you're able to comprehend. This may be true for those who only focus on the "speed" part of the speed-reading skill. But, again, if you learn how to do it properly, you will be able to do both at the same time.

Knowing how to speed read and when to speed read are important, but they're not the only bits of information which can help you out. Learning speed reading is a process wherein you need to keep on practicing if you want to achieve mastery. Here are some tips to help you as you start out:

- During your speed reading "study sessions," minimize distractions. Create an environment for yourself where there are very little to no distractions or interruptions. Such an environment will allow you to concentrate on what you're trying to learn and read.

- Start slowly and go easy on yourself. This is especially true if you don't see reading as a particularly enjoyable activity. Try to find simple articles or uncomplicated novels for your first speed-reading learning sessions. That way you won't feel overwhelmed once you start reading. Also, you'll understand what you've read more, which, in turn, will make you feel motivated to keep going.

- Sometimes it helps when you cover the text which you have already read. This will help you avoid going back to those words which might slow down your reading process.

- Before reading, think about what you want to learn from the material. This can be very useful, especially when you make use of the skimming method of speed reading. Knowing what you want to learn will prepare you for what you're about to read and force you to find the significant words, phrases or sentences.

- Keep track of your progress. This will help you determine if you're improving or not. You can test yourself, time yourself, or even use free speed-reading assessments which you can easily find online.

Feel Empowered

Each day, people judge you for every word you say; this gives them something to think about. So, in cases where you have to attend a business meeting or something equally important where you have to speak up, be sure that what you say is nothing but facts. To get these facts and be able to convey them confidently, you need to read and comprehend reliable resources. Speed reading can be very beneficial for this requirement, especially when you have to prepare yourself in a short amount of time.

Speed reading can also help you out in social situations. The faster you read, the more you will be able to read. And, if you also understand what you're reading well, you will be able to share that knowledge with the people around you. Keeping yourself updated with current news and events will make you feel confident. No matter what the people around you will talk about, you will be able to give your opinions based on what you have read.

In both situations and more, it's evident that speed reading can help empower you. So, no matter what type of situation you're in, you will be able to hold your own. You won't have to feel embarrassed when you're interacting with different kinds of people. Being a speed reader will make you an avid reader which, in turn, will give you the confidence you need to deal with everyone around you.

Improve Your Concentration and Memory

The more you practice speed reading, the more you will learn how to pay attention to what's discussed in the text. This, in turn, will help improve your concentration. And the more you focus on and understand the material you're reading, the better you will remember it. As your concentration improves, your levels of comprehension will also improve. This allows you to recall what you've read better, which means that, over time, you're able to retain more information effectively.

The fact is, properly learning how to speed read won't just increase your reading speed. It will also increase your comprehension. But we should emphasize that this will only happen if you learn the skill the proper way. Remember that speed reading isn't just reading speedily, it's also about being able to absorb the material, understand it, and be able to remember everything it says when you need to.

So, if you think that one of your weaknesses is concentrating on tasks at hand, learning speed reading can help you out, too, especially when it comes to reading. As you learn the skill, you will become more interested in what you're reading, no matter what type of material it is. Combine this with your eagerness to learn and you will definitely see how this improves your life in the long-run.

Improve Your Problem-Solving Skills

When you learn the skill of speed reading, you will be about to double or even triple the amount of reading material you finish given the same length of time. The more efficient you get, you may start realizing that you just have to skim through the material in order to comprehend what it says. Apart from this, speed reading also allows you to absorb more information and covey it to your subconscious. When this happens, your subconscious mind will get better, which, in turn, will also help you solve problems.

Reading is considered a brain exercise. So, when you do brain training such as trying to read at a faster rate, something incredible starts to happen. Eventually, your brain gets better at organizing information and making connections from what you're reading to what you already know. So, the more you hone your speed-reading skills, the more this process improves. You will then notice that your logic has also improved, allowing you to respond faster to situations and problems compared to how you performed in the past.

This is a very important benefit of speed reading because we are faced with problems every day. Whether you're a student, a stay-at-home parent, a professional, and more, you would have to deal with these issues at some point during the day. And if you're able to do so faster (thanks to speed reading), this will definitely be a great thing for you!

Move Forward in Your Career

Speed reading can also help you professionally. Each day, you probably go to work and see piles of papers on your desk and a bunch of unread emails in your inbox. These may come in the form of files, reports, memos, assignments, and more which need to read to accomplish all of your daily tasks. But, if you're a slow reader, or even if you read at a normal rate, you might not have time to do anything else!

For instance, there may be times when you went on a holiday for a couple of days or you didn't come to work over the weekend. When you come back, chances are that you have a lot of things to read to get you up to speed with what has happened while you were away. If those days when you were absent were particularly busy, you will have a lot to read about. Of if you're given assigned reading at work, which you're required to finish within a given time frame while still accomplishing your other tasks, speed reading also becomes an essential skill.

If you're an effective speed reader, you will find your work becoming lighter. You'll be able to breeze through those work emails, memos, reports, and other written documents. And, if you have to learn something new before going into a meeting, doing this won't be much of a challenge either. This skill will prove to be a huge factor in the improvement of your professional life.

Chapter 5

Speed Reading Mistakes

Learning how to speed read is a continuous process. You don't just decide that you want to speed read and then magically obtain the skill the next day. In fact, many people who start to learn commonly mistake speed reading with reading faster. Although this is essentially what speed reading is all about, we've already discussed how this skill is more than just reading faster. Some people may find success simply by reading faster, but this won't last for very long.

When you start learning how to speed read by reading the material faster without trying to understand it, you might lose interest in learning the skill, because this process can get exhausting really quickly. Yes, you're able to "read faster" but you don't actually understand what you've read. So, you have to keep going back to the text, reading it repeatedly until you finally get the point. This is what makes the process exhausting.

Most of the time, the process of learning how to speed read starts with some sort of visual training. Honing the efficiency of your eyes is an important part of the learning process. But this doesn't mean that you should take extreme measures when training your eyes. Also, if you focus too much on training your eyes, your mind might wander off, which renders your efforts meaningless.

Basically, if you want to become an efficient speed reader, you need to improve your reading performance, attitude towards reading, and learned reading behaviors. Speed reading doesn't just involve speeding up your visual processes. You should also improve the way your mind responds to the printed material. In other words, it means that you have to change how your eyes work and how you comprehend what you're reading.

When you think about it, the only change which occurs is a perception change. This refers to how your brain processes, filters, and interprets information. Right now, you have learned how to read a certain way. Your brain has been conditioned to read and interpret printed material in a pattern which involves reading one word at a time. This is one of the hardest habits to break, but it's not impossible. You must break this bad habit if you want to learn how to speed read correctly and effectively.

Simple as it is to describe what you need to change and improve, it does require a lot of conscious effort in reality. You may feel overwhelmed at some point, but keep pushing yourself and finding the motivation to keep yourself moving forward. The great news is that we will help you make the whole process easier by arming you with all the information you need to learn the skill of speed reading.

The Importance of Learning Speed Reading Correctly

When most people hear the word "muscle," they will most likely think about their chest or their biceps. These are some of the most common muscles exercised, and recognized by everyone. But what a lot of people don't remember (or know) is that the brain is a muscle too! And it's the most important muscle in our body, especially when it comes to speed reading. As we age, it becomes even more important to exercise our brains to keep them sharp and prevent them from deteriorating as much as possible. The great thing about our brains is that, even in our golden years, they will continue to relish the training, unlike our other muscles, which may end up becoming weaker with age. And one excellent way to maintain the health of our brain is to learn and practice speed reading.

Essentially, speed reading is a skill wherein you're able to read at an increased rate compared to "normal" while still being able to understand what you've read. Reading as fast as 1,000 words each minute is possible if you learn how to speed read correctly. This may sound too good to be true for some, especially for those who despise reading. Now it's time to learn the importance of learning this skill CORRECTLY.

- **You will see an improvement in your logical sequencing**

The more you speed read, the better your brain becomes at sorting, grouping, and organizing information. As you learn the correct speed-reading methods, your brain learns how to correlate information into meaningful thoughts at a much faster pace.

- **Your ability to focus will improve**

When you're tasked to read something, especially if you're not really interested in it, you'll notice how easy it is to lose focus due to your surroundings. You might receive a text on your cellphone, hear your favorite song playing on the radio, or see something interesting outside your window. There are so many things which can distract you while reading. But if you learn how to speed read properly, you are trained to focus on what you're doing in order to group the information and sequence it properly (remember active reading?). This, in turn, requires you to maintain a laser-like focus on the task.

- **Your memory capacity tends to increase too**

We've talked about how speed reading is an excellent form of brain training. And the more you train your brain, the greater your memory capacity will become. Think about it as your brain's version of becoming "bigger" and "stronger." Your mental capacity will grow as you learn the techniques of speed reading and practice them often.

- **You will enjoy a high sense of achievement**

When you're able to learn new skills, you receive a huge confidence boost. Think about it; when was the last time you learned something new? How did it make you feel? Most likely, as soon as you've realized that you have learned that new skill or information, it gave you a high sense of achievement. The same thing happens if you have learned speed reading and noticed how much it has enriched your life. This will even motivate you to keep going and learning new things and new skills.

Avoid These Common Speed-Reading Mistakes

Speed reading is an important skill. Although it was already considered an important skill in the past, it's even more relevant in this modern day and age. No matter who you are and what you do, speed reading will not only help you survive, but it will also help you thrive and move forward a lot easier. Speed reading involves more than just reading text quickly. There are certain methods you need to employ if you want to speed read successfully and effectively. To do so, it's important for you to avoid these very common mistakes:

1. You focus too much on the speed or on the mechanical side of speed reading

A lot of speed-reading approaches and programs tell you to "speed things up." Of course, this is an important part of the skill, especially at the beginning. But when it comes to understanding the material, you can only read as fast as your mind is able to comprehend. So, it's important to learn how to differentiate practicing the skill from applying it to the real world. This means that, although speed is an important aspect of speed reading, it's not the only thing that matters. Once you've achieved the speed, you should also learn how to achieve the performance.

Your eyes are the "mechanical tools" which you use to read. Again, these are very important when learning the skill. But never discount the importance of your brain. No matter how well you're able to train your eyes to read faster or more, if your mind isn't absorbing the information, you can't consider yourself skilled. So, you should place equal importance on the mechanical and cognitive aspects of the skill.

2. You're holding yourself back

If you want to be an effective speed reader, you should prepare yourself for the task. You need to perceive and think in new ways. A lot of times, beginners hold themselves back because they are still skeptical or they aren't able to change the way they perceive. Beginners may increase their speed a bit, but they don't continue with the "speed development" because they see that their comprehension is starting to suffer. A lot of people think that they will be able to understand what they're reading the same way they did in the past. But in reality, learning how to speed read will transform the way you perceive print and the way you process the information you absorb.

Another thing that may be holding you back is the level of effort you put into learning the skill. If you really want to become a speed reader, you must put in consistent effort every time. You can think of speed reading as a skill you need to learn and improve for the rest of your life. Unfortunately, a lot of people aren't really invested in the learning process, and they don't see it as "important." So, they put other things first time and time again until they've forgotten that they were trying to learn a new skill in the first place. Don't be one of these people. If you want to see the fruits of your labor, make sure to put in the effort!

3. You give up at the first sign of difficulty

As previously mentioned, speed reading is a skill which involves considerable time and effort. You have learned how to read a certain way and you have been reading this way all your life. In order to speed read correctly, you have to break a few bad habits and learn a couple of new ones. Depending on how you learn, you may experience a few bumps along the way. Don't get discouraged by challenges. Learn from them and don't give up at the first sign of difficulty. Keep thinking about the benefits and how this skill will enrich your life. In doing this, you can motivate yourself to stick with the process until you see your efforts pay off.

4. You expect perfection or mastery right away

This is one mistake which becomes the downfall of a lot of would-be speed readers. Speed reading is a skill. It's not a one-time learning concept which you will learn in a single session. For simple skills such as basic origami, tying simple knots, and more, you may just need one or two lessons to achieve mastery. But for speed reading, there's a lot for you to learn. The mechanical process of learning how to read faster takes time and practice. The comprehension aspect of speed reading takes time and practice, too. And when you start learning the different methods which will help you speed read, that's another process too. You need to learn all these things and learn how to apply them if you want to master the skill.

If you're expecting perfection from the beginning, you're setting yourself up to fail. Even if you've become an effective speed reader, that doesn't mean you've achieved perfection! You can always learn new things with a skill such as speed reading. So, immerse yourself in the learning process and take the word "perfection" out of your vocabulary so you won't end up frustrated with yourself each time you aren't able to learn as fast as you'd like to.

5. You try to do everything at the same time

For some people, they learn one method and they try to apply it to all types of material. For instance, they learn how to read a certain type of text and think that is the right way to read all other kinds of text. Of course, this isn't right. However, this is how we were taught to read in the first place! When you learn speed reading, you will come to realize that different types of text require different methods of reading. If you're tasked to read an informational material such as a journal article, you may need to focus more to get the meaning of what you're reading. By contrast, if you want to read a novel during your free time, you won't breeze through it just to get the main idea. You would want to read it at a slower pace (you should be able to control your pace better when you're a speed reader) in order to enjoy the story and immerse yourself in it.

These are the most common and most "dangerous" speed reading mistakes to avoid. There are others, too, such as:

- Trying to read every word so you "won't miss anything."

- Wanting to remember everything written in the text, no matter how irrelevant.

- Thinking that skimming is a form of "cheating."

- Going back to sentences or paragraphs which you have already read, even if there's no need to do this.

As long as you remember all of these speed-reading mistakes and catch yourself each time you make them, you will improve your learning process. The great thing is, when you're aware of the mistakes to avoid, you will be able to consciously realize if you're doing them and you can stop yourself.

Chapter 6

A Quick Rundown of
the Best Speed-Reading Techniques

It's finally time to learn more about speed reading, the essential skill. There are different methods to use when learning how to speed read properly. These include:

- Minimizing subvocalization;

- Word chunking;

- Using your peripheral vision;

- Hand pacing;

- Skimming and scanning;

- and so much more.

In the next few chapters, we will discuss these techniques and methods for you to understand them better and use them in your learning process. All of these techniques and more are important when you want to learn how to speed read correctly. Remember that speed reading involves much more than just reading at a fast pace. You also need to understand and remember everything you've read. Speed reading is a skill which will enrich your life. Practicing the skill to improve it helps you learn more about yourself and your abilities.

Different Techniques for Different Texts

Before we move on to the different speed-reading techniques, there's one more thing that you must understand. Unlike normal reading, speed reading works in different ways when you're reading different types of texts. For instance, if you read a text which contains a lot of facts and detailed information, you may have to take your time when reading. Whether you're a speed reader or not, such text requires more time and focus. Even though there are techniques which can help improve the speed of your reading, don't expect to go beyond twice your previous speed if you're reading these types of texts.

Scientific or legal texts that may depend on something as small as a turn of phrase require a slower pace. Otherwise, you might miss out on a few important things which may affect how you understood the material. If you're only reading the material for informational purposes, then this may not be a big deal. But if you're reading the material for a specific purpose, such as something which involves legality, then you really need to slow down and understand everything that's written.

But when you're reading fictional books, self-help books, and other "light" reading materials, you may go as fast as you can, especially if you're not really emotionally invested in what you're reading. With other texts which don't have a lot of details, such as non-technical magazines or newspapers, you can go even faster. For these types of reading materials, all you need is to understand their main topic to get the message.

From these examples, you can see that speed reading actually depends on physical reading methods and on the ways your brain processes the information it absorbs. This means that the more details the written information has, the more your brain needs to process that information. In such cases, your speed-reading skill might not be relevant as you need to slow down in order to understand EVERYTHING printed on the reading material.

One of the easiest ways for you to absorb an entire book quickly is to go through the table of contents. This part of the book provides you with a general idea of what's written in the book. It also allows you to see which are the most important chapters and which chapters only contain "general" information. You can use a similar technique when reading the chapters of a book, especially if they contain sub-headings. Reading these sub-headings provides you with a good idea of what the chapter is all about. Also, you will be able to determine which sections are relevant and which you only need to skim through.

One of the core methods of speed reading is to absorb more words at a time. To do this, you should first make sure that you don't have any problems with your eyesight. Sadly, there are a lot of people who think that, no matter how hard they try, they just can't learn the skill. But in reality, their problem is that they need a pair of glasses.

One quick tip which involves absorbing more words at a glance is to keep your reading material a specific distance away from your eyes. This makes it easier for you to see larger parts of it. Relax and allow your eyes to just flow smoothly over the page in different directions. In doing this, your mind will start absorbing the most relevant words and phrases on that page and place these in your memory. This is a simple tip you can use to speed up your reading. There are other methods to employ as well, which we will learn in a while.

Some Speed-Reading Strategies to Start You Off

There are plenty of reasons why people want to learn speed reading, for instance, if your job always involves a lot of paperwork and your deadlines are right around the corner or you're a student and you need to get through a lot of reading to prepare for your exams. For some people, they just want to improve themselves, which is why they learn the skill of speed reading. No matter what your reason is, learning this skill will definitely help your life. Now, before we start with speed reading techniques, let's have a couple of effective speed-reading strategies to start you off:

- **When training or practicing, use a timer**

One of the best ways to keep track of your progress is by using a timer. From the beginning, you can time yourself. That way, you know your reading rate when you started, and you know how much you're improving each time. Using a timer is an excellent way to test and challenge yourself as needed.

When you use a timer, you also need to record the timings you've clocked in. For instance, try reading an entire article while timing yourself. Then, after some time, test yourself by reading a similar article with the same length and see if you've become faster. You can also set a specific time on the timer and, once it goes off, check how much you've read or how many pages you've turned within the given time. Again, after some time has passed and you've learned the methods and have started practicing, test yourself and see how much you've improved.

Apart from testing yourself and recording your progress, you can also use the timer to challenge yourself. Each time you test yourself, try your best to beat your previous record. Every time you do this, it will keep you motivated to push forward and keep practicing.

- **Set personal speed-reading goals**

Once you've started your speed-reading learning journey, set personal goals for yourself. These don't have to be huge, challenging goals. You can set weekly or monthly goals to make it easier for you to achieve them. Setting goals also make you accountable for your own actions.

When you have these goals, you will feel more motivated to stick with what you're learning until you get better and you're able to reach the harder, more challenging goals which you have set for yourself. If you think it will help, you can reward yourself each time you've achieved one of your goals.

- **Practice reading... a lot!**

Do you remember the old saying, "practice makes perfect?" This actually makes a lot of sense, and it applies perfectly to speed reading. Anytime you're learning a new skill, you should keep practicing it if you want to improve. The same thing goes when you're trying to learn how to speed read. The more you practice the skill, the better you become at it. And the better you are, the faster you will read while still being able to understand what you're reading. Practice is an important part of the learning process, so never discount its importance.

- **Try to broaden your vocabulary**

We've discussed the importance of a broad vocabulary in the previous chapters, but this is worth mentioning again. It becomes easier for you to read and understand when you have a broad vocabulary. Think about it; when you're reading something and you're going faster and faster, you'd probably feel great about the momentum you've built. Then you encounter a word which you aren't familiar with and can't understand.

This will definitely make you pause. If you skip the word, you might not be able to understand the rest of the sentence. You can also try figuring out what the word means by how it's used in the sentence. But what if in the same sentence, there's another word you're unfamiliar with? What do you do then? Do you stop what you're reading and check the dictionary? No matter what course of action you choose to take, this will significantly slow down your reading time. In the case where you check the meaning of the word, this entails putting the book down, looking for your dictionary, and checking the definition.

This is why it's so important to have a wide vocabulary. The good news is that you can achieve this by reading more and more. As you read different kinds of materials, you will get introduced to a lot more words used in different contexts. If you keep adding words to your repertoire, you will be able to read faster. This is because you won't have to pause to think about or try to find the meaning of unfamiliar words. And the faster you're able to read, the more you will be able to read, too.

- **Skim the text to find the main points**

Skimming is one of the most important methods used in speed reading. This method is particularly useful if you need to go through a lot of material in a short amount of time. In such a case, don't panic. The more you panic, the less you will understand what you're reading.

When it's time to read, calm down, take a deep breath, and focus on what you're reading. Skim through the text and try to find all of the main points. If you're reading a book, check the table of contents first. Then for each chapter, read the sub-headings. If there are any illustrations or diagrams, read the captions quickly, too. Doing all of this will give you a general idea of what the text is all about.

After you've done this, it's time to read the first paragraphs of each of the main sections then read the last paragraphs. Finally, read the paragraph in the middle. Consider everything you've read and try to piece all of the information together as best as you can. This will give you more information about the material you're tasked to read. After that, you can begin reading the rest of the content while using speed-reading methods. Following this process will allow you to absorb and retain all of the information more effectively. It will also allow you to get through everything at a faster rate.

- **Set your mind to the task**

This is another effective tip for you to remember. Once you've started reading, you have to set your mind to the task at hand. This will help you become an active reader which, in turn, will help you increase your reading speed. One of the worst possible habits to have while you're learning how to speed read is daydreaming. Unfortunately, a lot of us can't stop our minds from drifting off as we're reading, especially if we're not interested in the material.

Once your mind wanders off, you won't be able to speed read effectively. If you notice that you end up daydreaming all the time, try turning this into something which will help you understand what you're reading better. The next time you catch your mind wandering away, try directing your thoughts towards the concept of the material you're reading. Try connecting the text with your own experiences. For instance, if you're reading a book about dealing with stress, try to think of times when you experienced a lot of stress. That way your brain will connect more to the material, which makes it easier to understand and remember.

- **Don't take reading too seriously!**

Finally, don't take the task too seriously! Yes, learning how to speed read involves a lot of time, consistency, and effort. But this doesn't mean that you should push yourself too hard. A huge part of learning how to speed read is to change your attitude towards reading. Try to think of reading as a fun activity rather than a chore. In doing this, you will have more fun while you're learning. And when you're having more fun, you'll notice that you're learning at a much faster pace, too. And now, on to the speed-reading methods which we've been mentioning over and over again!

Chapter 7

Speed Reading by Minimizing Subvocalization

B y far, this is the most important speed-reading method, and it also happens to be the most challenging to overcome. When you read, you are limited by how much time it takes your subconscious mind to vocalize the printed words. Even though you may not say these words out loud, you're vocalizing them in your mind unconsciously. This process is known as "subvocalization," and it's one of the "bad habits" you must break if you want to become a successful speed reader.

Think about this situation: you're reading sentences quietly, but you notice that your lips are still mimicking what it's like to say those words out loud. This is a perfect example of subvocalization. Unfortunately, this habit of saying the words as you read them is one you have learned from the beginning. This means that it's already profoundly embedded in your conscious mind that you don't know how you're supposed to break the habit!

Don't panic, though, because eliminating this habit is entirely possible. One trick you can do is select one word in printed material and stare at it for some time in total silence. In the beginning, you will still notice some level of subvocalization when you do this. But if you keep on looking at words without trying to pronounce them out loud or in your head, you will form a new habit. Although this tip may seem a bit abstract, having this feeling is totally normal. What you need to concern yourself with is looking at the words without wanting or needing to hear what they sound like.

Remember the importance of practice? This is one of the situations where you really need to practice. The more you practice, the more you will start noticing that there's a real difference between saying the words unconsciously, or in your mind, and just allowing the words to be absorbed by your mind. Don't stress yourself out too much as this step will take a lot of time and conscious effort. But once you're able to do this, you've broken down the hardest and most restricting barrier standing before you and your quest to learn speed reading. Compared to this step, learning all the other methods will seem like minor things. The good news is that in this chapter, we will learn how you can minimize this habit to help you learn how to speed read effectively.

Hearing Your Voice in Your Head

Subvocalization which is sometimes known as "auditory reassurance" is a habit that most readers have. This happens when you say the words you read in your head, and it's one of the biggest reasons why people aren't able to improve their reading speeds. Although it would be best if you can eliminate this habit completely, studies have shown that this isn't really possible. So, the next best thing you can do is to minimize your subvocalization, which, in turn, can help give your reading speed a boost. Doing this may also help improve your reading comprehension.

When most of us first learned how to read, we had to read the words out loud. After gaining proficiency, we had to learn how to read silently by saying the words in our heads. Basically, this is where subvocalization originated, in the basic process how we were taught how to read. For those who don't learn speed reading, they read through vocalization all their lives. Although this isn't the "wrong" way to read, this habit will hinder you from becoming an effective speed reader.

If you want to understand what you're reading, you don't have to say every printed word in your head. Although this may have been essential when you were still learning how to read, you should be able to get the meaning of the words just by seeing them. You should have the same level of comprehension when you read this way as when you say each of the words in your head.

Simply seeing words and understanding them is entirely possible. One great example applies to those who drive. When you see a sign which says "STOP," you won't really look at it and read the word in your head, right? As soon as you see this sign, you know that it says "stop" and you understand what it means. This is one concrete example of seeing a word and understanding it. This happens because you've learned what the word means, so whenever you see it, you already know what it means.

From this example, you can see that minimizing subvocalization is possible. All you have to do is consciously learn how to see words without saying them in your head and understand what they mean. Once you've learned how to do this, keep practicing the skill to hone it. Eventually, you'll notice that your subvocalization reduces. When this happens, you can start learning how to read at a faster rate.

What Happens During Subvocalization

If you were given the task to read text right now, you would probably do so the way you were taught in the past. Starting from the left side, you would read each word, phrase, and sentence one by one. When you reach the end of the line, your eyes would return to the left side of the page and repeat the same process. Then, as you're reading silently, you hear the words in your head, and, sometimes, you may even catch yourself mouthing the words as you read them.

This is the common way of reading and it's how most normal readers go through written material. Again, there's nothing wrong with this way of reading. As a matter of fact, it can be very effective for those who are just learning how to read. But, if you look at it as part of speed reading, then this subvocalization habit has no place. One reason it slows down your reading pace is that subvocalization involves too many parts of your body. You see, as you're subvocalizing, several things happen at the same time:

- Your eyes are occupied as they fixate on each of the words.

- Your mouth is occupied as its busy mouthing the words your eyes are seeing.

- Your mind is occupied as you're saying the words you're reading subconsciously.

- If you're reading softly, then your ears also become occupied as they try to listen to what your mouth is saying.

As all these parts of your body work together on a single task, your brain has to work even harder as it tries to process all of the input coming from your eyes, mouth, subconscious, and ears. At the same time, your brain is also trying to comprehend the text you're reading. This is truly a lot of work! And, since so many body parts are working for just one task, the process is quite inefficient.

Breaking the Subvocalization Habit to Improve Your Reading Speed

When you think about it, reading isn't just about the words printed or written on the page. It's more about absorbing the information, the ideas, and the details. Words don't have much meaning unless they appear side by side with other words to form ideas, messages, and concepts. For instance, if you read the words "World Health Organization," do you think of the meaning of each individual word? Most likely you understand these words together and know that they refer to the worldwide organization.

When it comes to written text, a lot of the words are just there for the purposes of correct grammar. These words aren't as significant as others, especially those which carry relevant meaning. As you minimize your subvocalization habit, you start with these common words. This will help give your reading speed a boost. The fact is, we don't have to read at the same pace as we speak. When you speak, you have to pronounce the words one at a time. But when you read, there are some words which you don't have to pronounce since they don't contribute significantly to the main idea.

Of course, minimizing the subvocalization isn't as easy as simply trying to read at a faster rate. Especially at the beginning, you will keep catching yourself reading the words one by one as you had learned in the past. It's not like this habit has an "off switch" which you can just flick to turn off in an instant. But, the more you practice, the better you will become at minimizing your subvocalization. Let's look at an example which shows the difference between reading with and without subvocalization.

For instance, you had to read a sentence saying, "The girl jumped over the hurdle." Right now, you may have read that sentence one word at a time. But when you've managed to minimize your subvocalization, the sentence may be reduced to "Girl jumped hurdle," which is a mere 3 words compared to the original sentence, which had 6 words. You're not actually skipping some of the words, you're just seeing them without saying them in your mind. This way, you're still able to understand what the sentence means without sacrificing your comprehension.

Tips to Help You Minimize Subvocalization

So, what happens when this habit changes? How would you know if it's changing or not? This is why it's important to test yourself from the beginning. You should know your current pace. After you practice staring at words without reading them for some time, try testing yourself again. If you discover that you're not reading each word one by one and you're able to read more words each minute, this means that the subvocalization habit is, indeed, changing. Apart from staring at words to learn how to internalize them instead of reading them in your head, here are more tips to help you minimize subvocalization:

1. Keep your mouth occupied while reading

This is one easy way to minimize subvocalization. If your mouth is doing something else while you're reading, this deactivates your brain's speech mechanism which, in turn, allows you to read directly with your conscious mind. When your mouth is busy, you don't have to unconsciously read the words with your mouth before your brain can process them.

So, how do you keep your mouth busy? One of the simplest ways to do this is to chew a piece of gum while you're reading. The act of chewing gum will keep your mouth and your vocal cords occupied so you don't end up mouthing the word's you're reading. If you can manage it, humming while reading can be quite effective, too. If you can this without compromising your reading, you'll notice that you're able to read faster almost instantly. Of course, this is just one tip to help you out, especially at the beginning.

2. Keep your mind distracted

We don't mean that you should do something else while you're reading. Otherwise, you might not be able to focus on your reading and this will slow you down. So, how can you distract yourself? One thing you can do is keep that voice in your head busy by forcing it to say other things. For instance, you can count in your mind as you're reading the printed material. As you do this, fixate on the different parts of the sentences.

So, what you will do is say "one" in your mind while looking at the beginning of the sentence or the line, say "two" while looking at the middle of the sentence, and say "three" while focusing on the end of the sentence. So instead of reading the words that you're looking at, you'll be counting in your head. The great thing about this is that you'll also learn how to fixate on groups of words instead of individual words.

You can either say these words softly or in your mind. Doing this will definitely keep you distracted so you don't read each word in your head one by one. Keep practicing and you'll notice that it becomes easier to say the words in your head without having to count. This, in turn, will help you read faster.

3. Listen to some music while you're reading

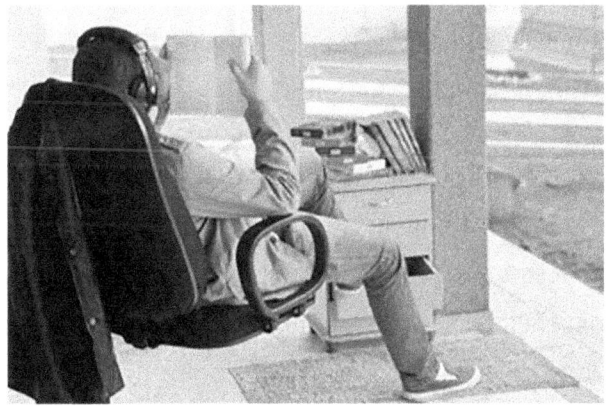

This tip helps you minimize subvocalization and it also helps improve your concentration. Of course, not all music types will work well for you. For one, you may want to stay away from upbeat music or those with lyrics as these might break your concentration once you start singing along. Also, try to avoid listening to music which you're emotionally connected to as these might make your mind wander to other things. The best kind of music to listen to is classical music or something instrumental. This will help with your concentration and may also help minimize your subvocalization habit.

4. Try to read at a faster rate every time you practice

Let's assume that you've started at a rate of 400 words each minute. When you're practicing, force yourself to read at a faster rate like 500 - 550 words each minute. This will help reduce the number of words you're saying in your head. Apart from helping minimize subvocalization, this tip will also improve your concentration and focus because you need to give more attention to what you're reading when you're trying to read faster. Once again, if you keep practicing and pushing yourself to read faster (along with employing the other methods), you will see your speed increasing and your subvocalization habit decreasing.

Subvocalization May Also be Beneficial

Of course, there are times when subvocalization can be beneficial. For instance, if you're reading a text which contains a lot of technical vocabulary or terminology which you aren't familiar with, saying these terms in your head or even saying them out loud can help you remember the words which, in turn, contributes to your vocabulary.

Another situation wherein subvocalization can be beneficial is when you need to memorize a text verbatim. Subvocalizing, or even saying each of the words out loud, will go a long way in determining how well you're able to memorize the text. This is one method actors use when they're trying to memorize all of their lines. Subvocalizing can help you with memorization, but when you're just reading something, you don't have to remember everything word for word.

Usually, the only reason you read something is to learn by absorbing the ideas, details, and information. So, when you want to be able to read at a faster rate, you don't need to practice the habit of subvocalization. Instead, you should minimize this habit as much as you can, so you're not limited by the words on the page.

Chapter 8

Speed Reading
Through Word Chunking

Once you've learned about speed reading, you'll become even more convinced that the pace you're reading at now isn't enough. This is especially true if you're a slow reader. It would take you a long time to get through a reading material, and this can be a challenge if you need to finish that material in a short amount of time. Slow readers don't like reading for pleasure, and when they're tasked to read an informative or technical text, they feel like it is such a heavy burden that will take them forever to finish. The good news is, you don't have to remain a slow reader. With the proper methods, you can learn how to become an effective speed reader.

The next method we will learn is word chunking. Most readers tend to read words one by one. Then, just like blocks, they piece the words together as they go through the sentence in order to understand what they're reading. But, if you want to learn speed reading, you must focus so you can see more words and chunk them together as you're reading. Rather than reading the words one at a time, group the words together and read them all at the same time. In the beginning, you can start by chunking two words at a time. As you practice and get better at word chunking, you can increase this number to three, four, five, and so on.

The Benefits of Word Chunking

Another excellent speed reading to learn is word chunking. This involves grouping or "chunking" words together as you're reading. This method differs significantly from how people normally read. This is because we were taught and trained to read one word at a time which, as we have pointed out repeatedly, makes us inefficient readers. Basically, word chunking involves combining a chunk or group of words together, allowing your brain to process them and comprehend them as a whole. When you combine this method with the other effective speed-reading methods, you will see yourself improving as time goes by. Let's take a look at the benefits of word chunking in terms of learning the speed-reading skill:

- **It helps you read at a faster rate**

Obviously, this is the most important benefit of word chunking. Since you combine the words together into meaningful chunks, you don't have to spend as much time as you would reading one word at a time. This speeds up your reading process and makes it more efficient.

- **It will help you understand what you're reading better**

When you think about it, the individual words in a sentence don't mean much. But, when you take these words together and allow your brain to process them as a group, your brain will be able to understand the meaning faster and better. For instance, if you see the words "Jane" "ran" "away," and you read them one at a time, your brain would have to process each word separately then bring them together in your mind to make sense of the sentence (or phrase). But if you group these words together and absorb them as "Jane ran away," your brain will immediately be able to understand what the sentence means. Then you can move on to other groups of words at a much faster rate.

- **Other benefits**

Word chunking is much easier to learn than the first method we discussed, which is the minimization of subvocalization. Still, it is a very beneficial method to learn. Here are the other benefits of learning word chunking:

- ✓ It's easier for visualize reading materials.

- ✓ It makes the other methods of speed reading easier and more effective.

- ✓ It can even help you minimize subvocalization.

- ✓ It helps you avoid going back to the previous words you've read as you are reading.

- ✓ It helps you comprehend the main idea with a single glance.

What is Word Chunking?

Word chunking is a clever method which helps you become a successful speed reader. But this method only applies to reading and not speaking. No one on the planet can say two, three, four or more words at one time. When we speak, we say the words one by one. And there's no way to change since trying to say several words at a time will just confuse the people you're talking to. But, when it comes to reading, word chunking is a way to look at several words, group them, absorb them, and let your brain process and understand them as a single entity.

If you learn how to chunk words while reading, you will transform from a turtle to a cheetah in terms of your reading speed. As you keep practicing word chunking, it will become automatic for you. Then you will be able to absorb more information in a shorter period of time. Whether you're a student, a professional or you just want to improve, word chunking will go a long way in helping you with your speed reading.

Of course, just like all the other speed-reading methods, word chunking requires a lot of practice. But, anyone who has good eyesight can learn this method. Basically, you will no longer see the words as separate elements. Instead, you start seeing them as groups of information to make it easier for your brain to understand. Your eyesight, though, is an important factor when you're learning how to word chunk. You need to use your 180-degree vision ability adequately if you want to chunk words. Connected to this method is the use of your peripheral vision, which we will be discussing more in the next chapter.

Word chunking also helps minimize your inner monologue, which is also known as the habit of subvocalization. Since you're seeing several words at once, you won't have time to pronounce those words in your head one by one. This shows how speed-reading techniques are all connected and how they help each other improve your reading speed.

Tips to Improve Your Word Chunking Skills

If this is your first time learning word chunking, start with two words. Don't feel bad when you're not able to chunk words right away. Remember, this is a method which requires practice. Keep practicing at the level you're in, and once you feel comfortable with it, you may try moving on to the next level. Here are the word chunking training levels for your reference:

- When you're at the beginner level, try chunking the words two at a time.

- When you're at the intermediate level, try chunking the words three to four at a time.

- When you're at the advanced level, try chunking words five or more at a time.

If you don't want to frustrate yourself, start learning how to chunk words slowly. There's no need for you to rush the process, especially if it ends up making you feel bad about yourself. Start by choosing a page of printed material to practice with. Then draw vertical lines on the page. Make sure that the lines separate the first two and the last two words in each of the lines on the page. This is an effective tip which trains your eyes to only focus on the middle part of the page. It also trains your peripheral vision to see the first and last two words on each line. Now, try to imagine that written lines have been divided into 3 phrases. If you can't imagine this at the beginning, that's okay. It's not a good idea to over-analyze. Simply read the section between the vertical lines you've drawn on the page and don't pay much attention to the outer words. This is a word chunking technique known as "triple-chunking," and once you've gotten used to it, you will read at a faster pace.

Keep practicing the triple-chunking technique until it becomes easy for you. When that happens, you can try to learn the "double-chunking" method. For this method, use the same tactics, only this time, divide the page into half instead of 3 parts. Then you start imagining that the lines only consist of two phrases. Look at one side of the page and try to "read" it as one group. Then look at the other side of the page and do the same thing. This method is a bit advanced, but, with enough practice, you can achieve this. Basically, these tips help reduce your fixations until you're able to remove them entirely.

Mastering the double-chunking technique is a mammoth task in itself. If you're able to do this, you will notice that you've increased your reading speed significantly. If you want to improve further, learn the "single-chunking" technique. For this technique, you will learn how to read entire sentences as if they were phrases. This method involves moving your eyes diagonally instead of moving them from left to right. You start by reading the right side of one sentence and the left side of another from the top of the page to the bottom while using a diagonal pattern of eye movements. This is an excellent method to speed up your reading, but you can only start with this once you're in the advanced level and you've mastered double-chunking.

Training Yourself to Read Words by Chunk

Most of us were taught how to read linearly: you pronounce each sound, each syllable, and each word one by one from beginning to end. This is an effective way to teach children how to read, but it's not a good practice for those who want to learn speed reading. Normally, you would fixate on each word and even say those words softly or in your mind before moving on to the next. But when you speed read, you should be able to minimize your fixation points in order to get through each sentence and line faster. This is known as word chunking or reading in saccades.

When you reduce the number of fixations you have on each line by grouping the words together, you will immediately increase your reading speed. To do this, you must commit to the task and build your own training plan which involves word chunking along with the other speed-reading methods. As a beginner, a reading session of about 15-20 minutes would be enough to improve your reading speed as well as your ability to simultaneously read and recognize chunks of words while reading. Here are some tips to help you out as you train:

1. Use the triple, double, and single-chunking methods

These methods involve dividing each line of text accordingly. Then you can start practicing your fixation by absorbing the words chunked together by the lines you've drawn. When using these methods, you can use a stylus, pen, or even your finger to guide you, especially at the beginning. Also, you may want to start with simple or light reading materials when you're starting out. When you notice that you're getting better and you're able to understand the text easily, only then can you move on to more complicated reading. These methods help extend your vision as well as reduce your regression and fixation.

The best way to begin word chunking is to start with only 2 words. This will help stimulate your brain and get it used to processing more words at a time. Rushing through the process or skipping levels isn't recommended, as you might just end up getting frustrated if you can't learn the method. What you can do while you're practicing on this level is to increase your speed if you want to stimulate your brain or slow down if you need to improve your comprehension.

One great tip you can try is to place your focus on the gap between the words. This will help you recognize two words better. Also, especially at the beginning of your training, limit your session to 15 minutes to give your eye muscles a chance to rest. Then, as time goes by, you can increase these training sessions little by little. Also, you might catch yourself subvocalizing often, especially at the beginner level. This is common, but you will be able to minimize this habit as you progress to reading more words at a time.

2. Combine word chunking with the other speed-reading methods

As previously mentioned, all of the speed-reading methods work best when you employ them alongside each other. For instance, during your training session, you can practice word chunking while chewing gum or listening to music (tips from the first method we've discussed). Using both methods will prove more effective as they will allow you to focus more on what you're reading. So, imagine how much better it will be if you also use the other methods?

3. Try to overcome all of the bad reading habits you've learned

Just like learning different speed-reading methods, overcoming your habits is easier said than done. BUT, it's not impossible. With the right knowledge and a lot of practice, you can break these habits and replace them with more effective ones, which will help boost your reading speed.

4. Learn techniques for visualization

There are plenty of visualization techniques out there. These will help train your eyes and make them stronger which, in turn, will make it easier for you to use your peripheral vision as you're chunking words and reading at a faster pace.

5. Ignore the "filler words"

We've discussed the words which exist in sentences just for the purpose of connecting them and making the sentences grammatically correct. Although these words are important, you can ignore them and still get the idea of the sentence. This is another great tip which will help increase your reading speed.

Chapter 9

Speed Reading
Using Your Peripheral Vision

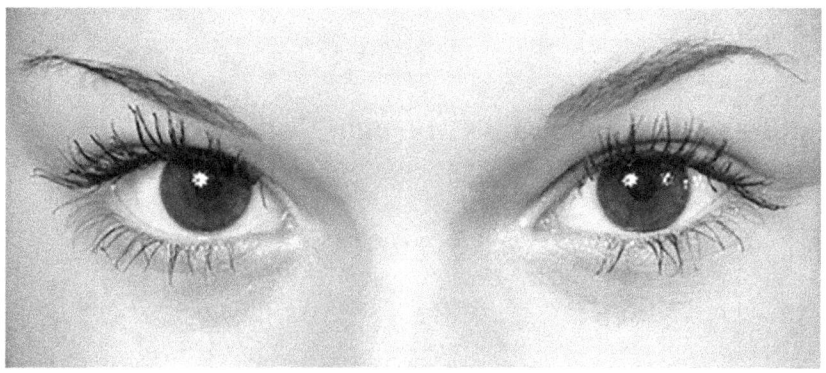

In line with word chunking, the next method to use for speed reading is using your peripheral vision. In fact, this method can help improve your word chunking abilities. Since you need to widen your vision in order to look at words by chunks, doing this will also help improve your peripheral vision. Eventually, you'll stop fixating on the individual words on the page as you will see more of what's written which, in turn, helps you read faster.

Your peripheral vision plays an important role when it comes to learning how to speed read. Peripheral vision is more than just what you can see in front of you. It also includes everything your eyes see around you and outside of the main area they're focusing on. For most people, their vision span isn't very wide, which means that their peripheral vision isn't well-developed. This is mainly because of how we have learned to read.

Since we've been reading the same way all our lives, we've never had a reason to expand our peripheral vision. But now that you realize that it's an important method of speed reading, you now have a very good reason to do it. Expanding your peripheral vision is important to see more of what you're reading and not just the words that you're chunking. In this chapter, we'll learn more about this method and how to do it, too.

Reading with Peripheral vs Macular Vision

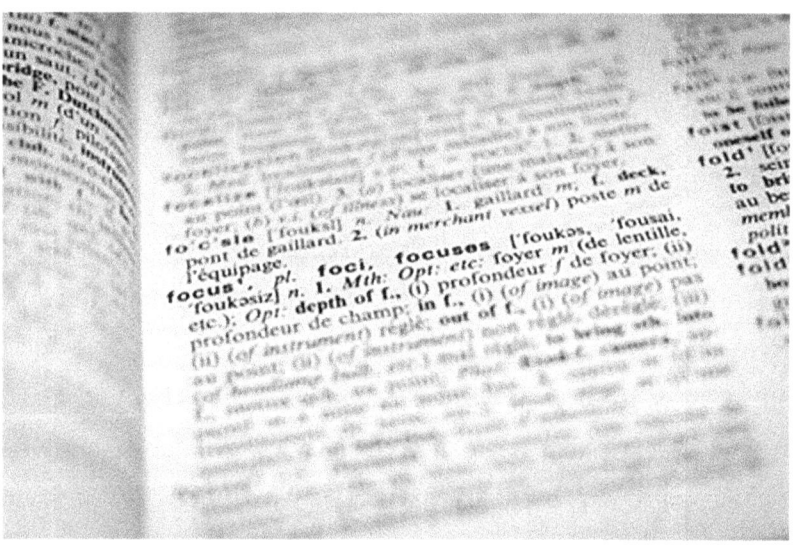

As previously stated, speed reading using your peripheral vision will be very helpful for word chunking. This method involves reading a group or "chunk" of words together with a single glance. Of course, as you do this, your reading speed increases compared to when you read the words one at a time. Doing this also minimizes your subvocalization: you can't say all of the words in each chunk at the same time.

The fact is, when you're reading text in columns (which is normally how printed text is presented anyway), you have a higher tendency to read in chunks. And the better you get at this method, the faster you will get at reading, too. Reading in chunks, or what's known as word chunking, is possible thanks to your macular and peripheral vision.

Macular vision refers to your main focus. When you're looking right at something, like a word, you're using your macular vision. On the other hand, your peripheral vision refers to everything else that you see outside of your macular vision. Normally, you see these things (or words) in less detail than the ones you see using your macular vision. Since your retina's receptor cells are concentrated at the middle of your eyes and not towards the edges, it's quite difficult to distinguish shapes and colors with your peripheral vision. Still, you can see the areas around your macular vision thanks to your peripheral vision.

As you're speed reading using word chunking, you use both your macular and your peripheral vision. With your peripheral vision, you can read while minimizing eye fixations. This is because your peripheral vision gives you a wider view, which means that you can see more words, read them, and process them at the same time. Rather than reading the words one at a time, you read a lot faster by chunking the words and processing them together.

But when you're reading through word chunking while also using your peripheral vision, you focus on the words in the middle (using your macular vision) and use your peripheral vision to see the other words surrounding the ones in the center. For instance, if you read a sentence which says, "Beauty is in the eye of the beholder," your macular vision sees the words "the eye of" while your peripheral vision sees the rest of the words on the left and on the right of these middle words.

How to Expand Your Peripheral Vision

The simple answers to this are practice and exercise. Each day, from morning until night, your eyes are occupied with everything you see. They're receiving a lot of visual stimuli, and they're constantly focusing then refocusing on whatever you want them to look at. Even as you're reading this book, your eyes are working without you even realizing it.

The six muscles attached to your eyes are doing most of the work. These muscles are responsible for controlling all of your eye movements, including the ones which make your eyes see all around you. These eye muscles also allow your eyes to focus on objects right in front of you and far away. These movements happen involuntarily. And the only times you notice their movements is when you're feeling eye strain. When your eyes water, you experience a burning sensation in your eyes, and your eyes twitch, these are some signs of eye strain. And when you feel them you should give your eyes a break.

Just like the other muscles in our body, exercise can help your eye muscles become stronger and more flexible. And just like the exercises which are meant to strengthen your different muscles, there are specific exercises which can help train your eyes to make them stronger and more flexible. One effective way to increase your eye strength is through exercise. The stronger your eye muscles become, the longer they can keep working before they get tired. And the more flexible your eyes become, the wider your peripheral vision becomes, too which, in turn, allows you to see more.

Here's one exercise you can do to train your eyes. Start by sitting or standing still. Then focus on a point directly in front of you. Then stretch out your arms to your sides as if pretending you are an airplane. Stick your thumbs up and maintain this pose. While keeping your head looking forward, move your eyes to the left until you're able to see your left thumb. If you're not able to see your thumb, just move your eyes as far as you possibly can. Then repeat the same procedure, but this time, move your eyes to the right. Do this exercise ten times for each side.

The Importance of Expanding Your Peripheral Vision

Your peripheral vision gives you the ability to see motion, objects, colors, and more outside of your macular vision. If you want to learn the skill of speed reading, it's important for you to train and expand your peripheral vision. Doing this will allow you to develop a broader eye-span. This allows you to read chunks of words at a single glance. The fact is, although reading words one by one isn't very meaningful. So, reading through word chunking helps you understand what you're reading better. To do this, some people even use wide-angled eyeglasses.

We've gone through the method of word chunking. Through this, you can read words 2, 3, 4, 5 at a time or more, depending on how much you've practiced and what level of word chunking you have reached. Your eyes fixate on groups of words which, in turn, increases your reading speed. This method shows that it's actually possible to read faster while still understanding your reading since your brain is actually absorbing the words as you're seeing them. With practice, you will also discover how wide your angle of view is. Over time, you will be able to read groups of words, making you a fast and effective reader!

The fact is exercises which expand your peripheral vision give your reading speed a boost. While you're focusing on a group of words, you'll still see the other words on the page, absorb them, and be able to understand what they mean.

Using Your Peripheral Vision to Improve Your Speed-Reading Skills

A lot of people are able to increase their reading speed by using their peripheral vision. With this method, they discover that their reading becomes better, and they're able to understand the text more, too. Another great thing about this method is that it improves your ability to concentrate. To make sure that the method is working, you may want to test yourself at the beginning first, even before you try employing any of the methods. That way, you will see how you're progressing and how quickly you're improving.

You may also want to "open up" your peripheral vision first before you read through a simple method. First, close your eyes. Then try to focus on a point around 15 centimeters above and a bit behind the top of your head. Even though your eyes close, you will feel your eyes soften as this makes your peripheral vision open up. Then take a moment to think about the material you're planning to read and what you want to get from it. Finally, breathe in deeply, and, as you're exhaling, open your eyes. After this, you can start your reading session.

While you're reading, you don't have to keep focusing on this point. But when you realize that you're losing your concentration, take a break from your reading, breathe in, then re-focus once again before you continue with your task. This is another method you must keep practicing if you want to improve your concentration and widen your peripheral vision. As time goes by, this will become easier for you.

Focusing on a single point known as the "point of concentration" will open up your peripheral vision automatically. This method doesn't just work for when you're trying to learn how to speed read. You can also do this before you drive, as it makes you more aware of your surroundings along with the other people and cars on the road. You can also do this before you take a walk when it's dark outside, as it will make you more aware of your environment. You can even perform this method before taking an exam to make yourself relax and allow yourself to remember things better, or anytime you think that you need to concentrate more on the task you're about to do.

When you first learned how to read, your teacher or parent taught you to read the words one at a time. This is a very effective technique for those who are just beginning to learn how to read. Unfortunately, a lot of people stick with this method until they grow up, hence, it's how they read all their lives. But we've already established that this isn't efficient, especially for speed reading.

The truth is, our brains are able to process a lot more information than just one word at a time. In fact, your brain can comprehend chunks of words, phrases, and even entire sentences. Anything that your eyes are able to see, your brain can process all at the same time. This is why you're able to respond to emergencies quickly. When such situations happen, and you see them coming, your brain takes everything in and tells you how to respond accordingly.

There's a way for you to test how many words you can read at a glance using your peripheral vision. You can use this test to determine how well your peripheral vision performs. To do this, select a word somewhere in the middle of a text (you can do this right now). The word must be in the middle of one of the lines of text and it must have a couple of lines above and beneath it. Focus on the word you've picked with both your eyes and try to see how many words you can still see and recognize clearly without moving your eyes. On your first try, you can probably recognize a few words surrounding the one you're focused on, depending on how long the surrounding words are.

Now that you have a better idea of how your own peripheral vision works, it's time to start practicing. The best type of material to use for practicing are standard paperback novels. Use your finger or a pen to select a word somewhere in the middle of the page. Then try to read the whole line with your peripheral vision. Unlike the first level of word chunking, this exercise is a bit more challenging. It's also more difficult than forcing yourself to read at a faster rate. So, don't force yourself. As you're starting to practice this method, start slowly. In fact, most people even end up reading at a slower pace, especially at the beginning. What you're trying to do here is train your mind to read entire lines of text at a time. And this is definitely a task that you won't be able to acquire overnight.

The more you practice, the better you will get at reading chunks of words at a time. You won't have to read the words one by one and pronounce them in your mind or softly with your mouth as you're reading. You will be able to just glance at the lines of text and allow your mind to absorb them all in one go. Try to practice this method with about 4-5 pages of text then take a break to give your eyes and brain a chance to rest. After that, you can continue with your practice and read another set of pages. Do this about 2-3 times each session, and soon, you will notice that you're getting better at reading lines of text rather than words of text at a time.

Mastering this method will take a lot of time and practice, especially since this is a whole new way of reading compared to how you have been reading since you first learned the skill. Just trust in yourself, your brain, and your own ability to learn how to train your peripheral vision effectively. Once you're able to master this method, you will discover how powerful it is and how it will help you understand what you're reading at a much faster rate.

Chapter 10

Speed Reading
Through Hand Pacing

The next method to learn about is speed reading through hand pacing. This is when you use your finger as a guide while you're reading. Most people think of this method as something children do when they're first learning how to read. That's why they stop doing it as soon as they become more proficient at reading. But, if you plan to learn speed reading, this method becomes very handy for a couple of important reasons.

One of the most significant challenges in learning how to speed read doesn't involve the actual learning process. Instead, the more difficult part is unlearning the old habits and skills we have learned in the past and which we are using now. Reading without hand pacing is one habit that will work against you when you're learning how to speed read. If you want to learn quickly, using your hand as a guide is very important. It's a non-negotiable habit to employ.

If you try to observe people who are speed reading, you may not see them using their hands to guide their reading. But what you will notice is that their eyes are darting from the start to the end of each line in a consistent pattern. And they are doing this at a consistent speed. Simply put, the time it takes for them to read one line of text is relatively the same for all the lines of text on the page. Probably the only exception to this happens when they suddenly get an idea from what they've read, or they get confused by an unfamiliar word. But these are normal parts of the reading process.

Hand pacing is an effective and essential method to employ, especially at the beginning of your speed-reading journey. You use your hand as a guide when you're reading, and the main goal of this method is for you to move your hand at a consistent pace. This trains your eyes to read at a consistent pace as well. As you're guiding yourself, you shouldn't slow down your finger or stop it at any point. You should be sliding your hand from one side to the other at a consistent speed. In doing this, you'll notice that it's easier for you to lose your momentum or get stuck at some point without your hand guiding you. But, when you're following your guide, concentrating on what you're reading and maintaining a uniform pace is much easier.

If you're just forcing yourself to read quickly, you might not be able to maintain a flowing and fluid pace, which is required for speed reading. This is because, at some point, you tend to skip a word, stop for a moment or even reach your limit. This, in turn, forces you to backtrack which, in most cases, makes you confused. Even if you just backtrack 2 or 3 times on each page, this adds a lot of time to your reading when the numbers add up. Then you'll end up losing a lot of time for each book you're reading, just because of backtracking!

This method is called hand pacing because most people use their fingers as the pointer which guides them. Using your finger makes a lot of sense because you have your finger with you at all times. Rather than using a pen or a stylus, which you would have to look for provided it's not right in front of you, merely placing your finger on the page takes no time at all. As you start reading, move your finger from left to right while absorbing the chunks of words on the page. You may notice that this method slows you down at the beginning (much like all the other speed-reading methods) but with practice, you will be able to read faster and more effectively.

When you've reached a more advanced level of speed reading, you can use the hand pacing method to increase your speed even more. To do this, keep your pointer about a centimeter or two away from the borders of the material you're reading. By this time, your eyes will be able to absorb and recognize words at a 1-inch radius; you don't have to point to the start of the line or reach the end of it.

What is Hand Pacing and Why Does This Method Work?

Hand pacing is a very effective speed-reading method which will help increase your speed and improve your reading comprehension. The best part about this method is that it's very easy to learn: we've used it in the past when we first learned how to read. Hand pacing involves using your finger as a pointer to guide you while you're reading.

A lot of people claim that this method is the fastest way for you to improve your reading performance. Combine this with the other methods we have already discussed, and those we will be discussing in the next chapter, and you'll surely become an effective speed reader in time. Hand pacing can help improve your focus, too while allowing you to skim reading materials first to get an overview of what you're about to read.

When some people learn what this method is all about, they may raise their eyebrows. This is because they may believe that this method is only for children and for those with reading disabilities. Of course, there's no truth to these beliefs. The fact is, this method helps you learn how to read faster the same way it helped you learn how to read in the first place. This method helps keep you focused on what you're reading, thus, allowing you to understand it better and remember more of it. It's a simple technique which involves moving your index finger along the lines of text at a speed that you're comfortable with.

As humans, we have a natural tendency to detect objects which are moving. This is why hand pacing is so effective. Let's clarify this point with an example. Try to imagine yourself watching television in your living room while sitting on a chair right next to a window. No matter how focused you are on what you're watching on the TV, if something moves outside and you catch the movement with your peripheral vision, your natural instinct would be to look outside to see what caused the movement. This is a tendency that we all have.

In fact, our ancestors had this tendency, too, as they needed to be able to detect even the faintest of movements in order to survive. We can make the most of this inherent skill through the method of hand pacing, so we can learn how to read faster. As your hand moves on the page, you are drawn to that movement. You focus on the movement of your hand and on the words that your finger is pointing to. And as you move your hand faster, your reading speed becomes faster as well. It's that simple!

No matter how fast you are at reading now, using the hand pacing method will definitely be beneficial for you. Slow readers, fast readers, passive readers, and active readers will find their reading performances improved when they employ this method. As you're practicing, train your eyes to coordinate with your hands so they can move more smoothly across the page. This will help you change any existing bad eye movement habits that you have learned in the past.

The Benefits of the Hand Pacing Method for Speed Reading

Using the hand pacing method to guide your eyes as you're reading will give an instant boost to your current reading speed. As we've discussed, the main reason for this is that your eyes are naturally drawn to movement which, in this case, is the movement of your hand from the start to the end of each line of text. When you use your finger as your pacer, you will improve your reading performance as it guides your eyes from start to finish. All you need to do for this method is to move your hand from the left to the right, going through one line at a time.

The hand pacing method is very effective because it helps improve your focus, too. Nowadays, with the advent of smartphones, gadgets, social media, and other distractions, it's becoming increasingly difficult to remain focused while you're reading. Some see these distractions as a curse which only exist in this modern time. Think about it; how easy was it to focus on reading about 100-200 years ago when there was nothing else to do but read? You didn't have to deal with having to answer phone calls or text messages. Neither were you compelled to check your Facebook feed to see what everyone else is up to. Back then, you would have gone through an entire book in no time. But now, with so many things to do, getting through a single reading is a huge chore!

Fortunately, you can learn how to speed read through different methods. And the great thing about these methods (including hand pacing) is that they can not only help you read faster, they also help you learn how to focus more on what you're reading. Focus is a vital part of speed reading. Without it, you won't be able to understand what you're reading anyway, no matter how fast you're reading. Here are the other benefits of the hand pacing method:

- it helps improve your reading comprehension

- it helps to give your reading speed a boost

- it guides your eyes as you're reading

- it helps improve your retention

- it helps improve your reading flow

- it helps reduce regression

- it helps train your mind to focus on what you're reading, even when there are distractions in your environment

- it saves a lot of energy and time

Simple as this method is, it's extremely effective, and the reason for this goes back to our natural tendency to detect motion. As you're guiding your eyes through the page, they are automatically drawn to what your finger is doing because of the movement. Whether you use your finger or another object as a guide, this method will be very helpful, especially when combined with minimizing subvocalization, word chunking, using your peripheral vision, and the other speed-reading methods we have yet to talk about.

Steps to Follow for the Hand Pacing Method

Ideally, the hand pacing method involves a number of steps to be performed properly. Don't worry, though, these steps aren't difficult because the hand pacing method itself is very simple. Hand pacing is very valuable when you're learning how to speed read. And it works even better when you keep practicing and combining it with the other methods.

There are different styles and moves you can use for hand pacing as you guide your eyes across the page, but you may only use these variations once you've mastered the most basic method of hand pacing techniques. To help you out, here are the steps to follow for the proper hand pacing method:

- Sit comfortably, turn your chair 45-degrees, and place your elbows on the table.

- Use your free hand to hold your reading material such as a magazine or book.

- Use either your right or left index finger as a pointer for this method.

- Place your index finger under the first word of the line then move along the first line at a pace you're comfortable with (you can increase your pace later on).

- Keep moving your finger while you're reading; once you finish the line, go to the beginning of the next line.

Repeat these steps until you reach the end of the text. Your index finger will determine your focus area as well as your speed. As much as possible, try to maintain a fluid and smooth motion while you're reading. You can either slow down or speed up as you try to maintain a good level of comprehension. If you happen to miss a couple of words, just keep going. You can deal with such an issue using the other speed-reading methods.

Additional Tips for the Hand Pacing Method for Speed Reading

Of course, the hand pacing method isn't just about moving your finger (or a tool) underneath the text. You should also train your eyes to follow your finger as a guide. This may be the simplest speed-reading method to learn, but you still need to keep practicing it to get better. In the previous section, we went through the steps to follow for the basic hand pacing method.

Stick with this method for some time until you see an improvement in your reading speed and how well you're able to follow your finger. Once you're familiar with the method and you find it "easy," you may move on to the variations of the hand pacing method. No matter which of these variations you try, make sure that you keep practicing the hand pacing method each day, along with the other methods. Set aside a couple of minutes for your training sessions each day if you want to see an improvement in your speed. Here are the variations of the hand pacing method you may try after mastering the basic technique:

- **Card method**: Instead of using your index finger or a pointer to guide you, use a card. This is more effective for some people as it helps them focus more and keep their eyes on the material they're reading.

- **Hop method**: For this variation, you will use four fingers instead of just one. This means that you would be looking at 4 words at the same time as you're reading. It's very helpful for when you've moved to the more advanced stages of word chunking.

- **Sweep method**: For this variation, you will cup your hand as you move across the lines instead of using a single finger. It's as if you're dusting off powder from the page as you sweep your hand from left to right.

- **Zig-zag method**: This is the most advanced variation to use, and it's only recommended after you've mastered the basic technique as well as the other variations. Here, you will move your finger diagonally for about three lines or so then go back. This allows you to scan more of the reading material in a single swipe.

When it comes to hand pacing, you should also learn how to control your speed. For instance, if you're reading detailed, informational text, then you may want to slow down. But, whenever you think you can, you may speed up as this will also help minimize subvocalization. As you perform this method, you're encouraging your brain to work faster in processing the words.

Chapter 11

Speed Reading
Through Skimming and Scanning

By now you have already learned most of the speed-reading methods you need to start your speed-reading journey. The previous methods we have discussed are important for you to understand the basic skills you need for speed reading. Just keep practicing them and you will be on the right track to becoming an effective speed reader. But we're not done yet. In this chapter, we will discuss the final method you need for your speed-reading skills.

If you want to learn the essential skill of speed reading, you must also learn how to skim and scan through all of the words in any reading material. Just like all the other methods we've learned, this skill comes with a lot of practice. But when you stick with it, you'll find it becomes easier as each day passes. Skimming and scanning reading material involves going through the text quickly from start to finish. The main purpose of learning this method is to get an overview or the main idea of the material before you read it as a whole. Learning this method is very important, especially if you need to get the gist of the material in a very short time.

What is Skimming?

The process of skimming involves quickly moving your eyes over an entire reading material to get the main ideas and the most important information. When you're trying to get an overview of the material you need to read, and it comes in the form of a book, you may skim through the table of contents, the summary of each chapter, the titles and subtitles of the chapters, the text passages, and any bulleted lists.

Skimming is actually a basic method of reading. The main objective of skimming is for you to familiarize yourself with the material as quickly as possible. You can apply this method for different types of material such as articles, books, newspapers, and more. Basically, you leaf through the text and look at the most important parts, such as the titles, illustrations, subheadings, charts, maps, and so on. Essentially, you're trying to understand the overall subject matter of the material you're about to read. This is important because reading speed and reading comprehension depend hugely on familiarity.

The more familiar you are with the material, the more comfortable you are once you start reading. And the more comfortable you are when you start, the faster you will get through the material and the more information you will be able to retain. Ideally, you would only need a couple of minutes to skim through the material in order to get an idea of what it's all about.

You can also use the skimming method to search for specific sections or passages which you may have missed or need to go back to. Use your eyes to go over the text to search for clues which will help you find these lost passages. No matter how "lost" you feel about the material, skimming through it will help refresh your memory until you find the text you need.

Another situation where skimming is effective is when you need to identify the material's main idea in a short amount of time. For instance, if you're reading a newspaper, you probably won't read it one word at a time. Rather, you would skim or scan through the text to get the main idea. This method works a lot faster than the normal way of reading. Therefore, it's essential when you need to go through a bunch of reading materials and you don't have enough time to finish everything.

Skimming and scanning are two different things. Skimming helps improve the skill of speed reading as it will help you look through a whole text quickly in order to get an overview of what it's all about. On the other hand, scanning is when you look through the text in order to find a specific bit of information. Use this method when you need to find the answer to a question. So, when you're scanning through a material, you have a couple of keywords in mind and you keep reading until you find them.

The Purposes of Skimming and Scanning for Speed Reading

Skimming and scanning are reading methods which involve the rapid movements of your eyes. When you skim or scan through text, you move your eyes quickly while searching for specific information, though you would use them for different purposes. Skimming is beneficial if you need to get a general overview of the text you're reading. Conversely, scanning is beneficial if you need to locate specific information. In other words, skimming gives you an idea of the information within the text while scanning helps you find a specific piece of information such as facts. Let's take a look at the purposes of these reading methods in order to understand them better:

Skimming

Skimming saves you time as you'll still be able to understand the material without having to go through hours of reading. Of course, this isn't always the "best" way to read in every type of situation. You can use this method to preview the material before you read it just to familiarize yourself with it first. After skimming, you will read the material at a faster rate because you already have a good idea of what it's all about. Then, as you're reading it, you may discover some important information that you might have missed when you skimmed over it.

You can skim over a material if you want to determine whether you need to read it or not. For instance, if you need to do research and you're searching for reading material, you can skim through the books, articles, and more first to see if they're worth your time. After getting a good idea of what the materials are all about, then you can decide whether you will read them thoroughly or not.

When you're skimming, go through the material quickly. You don't have to read each of the words, just pay attention to the most important information, such as keywords, names, dates, and even typographical cues, and text which has been formatted differently than the rest. When it comes to skimming, here are some basic steps to follow:

- If the material has a table of contents, skim over it. Also, read the chapter overviews to learn more about what they contain.

- Look at the main headings of each of the chapters, subheadings, tables, and charts.

- Read the whole introductory paragraph of each section. For the next paragraphs, only read the first and last sentences.

- Quickly go through any sentences which contain keywords formatted in italics or boldface.

- If you think you've discovered something important, take a moment to read the whole sentence, then continue skimming over the rest of the text.

- If there are any chapter summaries, read them too.

Scanning

Scanning also involves looking for organizational cues and keywords. But, unlike skimming, the goal of scanning is to locate and identify specific information. For different kinds of reading material, the facts are usually buried within the paragraphs. When you're doing research, you need to find these facts without having to read everything else. So, before scanning, you may want to skim over the material first to determine whether it contains the information you need. When you're scanning through text, know exactly what you're looking for. To scan effectively, follow these basic steps:

- Before you start scanning, think about the keywords or phrases that you need to find.

- Make a list of these keywords and phrases then only search for them one at a time. If you need to find several facts or bits of information, scan the material several times, too.

- Allow your eyes to float quickly over the text until you find what you're looking for.

- When you see one of the keywords or phrases you're looking for, stop and read the sentence which contains it.

- If you need to find an answer to a question, think about the keywords first before scanning.

- If you think you've found the answer, confirm this by re-reading the question to understand it better.

Unlike skimming, scanning requires more focus. So, keep practicing this method until you're able to do it without getting distracted. If you're finding it hard to do, you may want to do your scanning in a place which doesn't have any distractions.

When Should You Skim Through Text?

Speed reading is a skill which allows you to absorb printed information at a much faster rate. But, in some cases, you just need to understand the main idea of the text without having to read the whole thing. This is where skimming can be very helpful. Skimming can also improve your speed reading because it teaches you how to move your eyes rapidly as you go over the text. However, skimming isn't applicable all the time.

When you're skimming, you get the most important information from the text without having to read all of the words and details. Go through the material, absorbing the keywords and sentences, to give yourself an idea of what the text actually says. The best time to do this is when you need to understand a text and you don't have the time to read it. You can also use this method when you need to determine whether or not the reading material will help you out.

Unfortunately, since skimming can triple or quadruple your reading speed, it doesn't do much in terms of improving your reading comprehension. So, you shouldn't skim through everything you need or want to read just to say that you're an "excellent speed reader." Here are some of the best times you can apply this method:

- **When you're reading material about topics you're already familiar with**

This often applies to articles about topics you're already familiar with, especially the really long ones. This is a good time to skim because it doesn't really make of sense to read the same material repeatedly. So, what you can do is to skim over these articles (or any other materials) just to identify the most important points. You can also skim through the material to find the most interesting parts or to find information which is totally new to you. But, if the text has a lot of interesting points, you may want to read everything from start to finish.

- **Before you read a material (and after)**

This is probably the best use for the skimming method. Skimming allows you to preview the material to get an overall idea of it in order to understand it better as you're reading. When you skim, your level of comprehension significantly increases which, in turn, makes your learning more effective.

It's also helpful to skim the material after you've already read it. This allows you to review the information you've read and remember it better. In doing this, you will also make sure that you have understood everything you've read. You might even find important information that you have missed while reading.

- **When you need to read a lot of materials and you don't have enough time**

If you find yourself in a situation where you need to read a lot of materials and you don't have enough time to get through everything, skimming can be a lifesaver. It will make a huge difference when you know the main ideas of the subject rather than not knowing anything at all. Also, when you skim, you will find out the most important materials you need to go through. In doing this, you will be able to "read" everything you need to in the time given.

Tips for Skimming and Scanning Effectively

Basically, skimming is all about looking through a text rapidly to understand its gist. Skimming is a speed-reading method which means that, with practice, you can become better at it. Skimming can also help you comprehend the material you need to read better as you're already reading. Of course, when you only skim the material, that doesn't mean that you've understood it completely. It's just a way of understanding the main idea without having to read the entire text. If you want to master the method of skimming, follow these tips:

- **Read whole introductions**

When it comes to introductions, authors put a lot of thought into them. They do this because the introductory paragraphs are the best places to explain what the rest of the material is all about. The introductory paragraphs are also where the readers get hooked on the material. So, when you're skimming, it is very helpful for you to read entire introductory paragraphs or chapters to get a better idea about the rest of the content. This is an excellent way of creating a foundation to connect everything else you absorb through skimming.

- **Find the formatting**

When it comes to reading materials, especially those which are meant to inform, authors make use of formatting elements to highlight the most important parts. Keep an eye out for these elements, as they're very important when you're skimming. Look out for italic or bold text, indenting, ordered or bulleted lists, and so much more.

- **Read the first sentences of each of the paragraphs**

The first sentence of a paragraph is known as the "topic sentence." Authors put a lot of thought into this sentence to hook the readers and give them a better idea of what the rest of the paragraph contains. So, if you read the first sentences of each paragraph, you will gain a better and more consistent understanding of what the material is all about. You may also want to read the last sentences, especially for longer paragraphs because they're meant to summarize the content of the paragraphs for the reader to understand them better.

- **Look out for any illustrations, images, captions, tables, and charts**

While you're skimming, take a moment to study any illustrations, images, captions, tables, and charts if the material has any of these. Then read the captions fully as they describe what these elements are about. Usually, captions are very short anyway, so reading them won't take a lot of time. These elements are very helpful, especially when they're in informative or technical reading materials. So, making them part of your skimming process may help improve your comprehension.

- **Calm down and skim**

If you're running out of time and you still need to get through a ton of reading material, don't panic. When you panic, your comprehension levels will decrease even more. In such cases, you need to calm down, take a deep breath, and skim over the materials instead of reading them rapidly sans the comprehension. Read the table of contents, all of the main points, headings and subheadings, captions, and more to get the gist of the material.

Keep all of these tips in mind as you're skimming to make sure that you're doing it effectively. And as you're reading the important information, try to connect everything in your head. After you've skimmed through everything and you discover that you still have some time to spare, read the rest of the content while employing the other speed-reading methods we've already discussed. Together, all of these methods will help increase your reading speed without sacrificing your comprehension and your ability to retain most or all of the information you've just read.

Chapter 12

Other Tips and Techniques
for Speed Reading

We've already gone through the most important methods to use when you're learning the skill of speed reading. Now let's take a look at some other helpful tips and techniques which may enhance your learning experience. Before that, find a book that you've read in the past. Make sure that it's one you would like to read again. The point of this exercise is to train yourself to read at a faster pace. Since you've already read the book, you already know what it's all about, and it will be easier to go through the text faster this time around. This is one way to practice your reading speed (just the speed). When you do this, you're essentially conditioning your mind to keep up with how fast you're reading.

As you're reading the book, you may notice that, while you're reading, your eyes will start chunking words together rather than reading them one at a time. Your eyes do this because they're already familiar with the text. And since your brain already knows what to expect from the text, it wants to get through the material faster. This is one great tip you may use when you're practicing the word chunking method. It trains you to group words together in chunks while minimizing your fixations.

This tip also helps you learn how to prioritize. We've talked about how all kinds of reading materials contain information which is both relevant and irrelevant. Focus on the more important information when you're speed reading. Again, since you already know the information in the book you've read in the past, you know on which parts of the book you'll concentrate more. This practice conditions your mind to do the same thing, even when you're reading new material. Whether you're employing this tip or the others we have discussed, set aside 15 minutes or so for your training sessions to learn speed reading. You can practice the methods one at a time (especially when you're just beginning to learn them) or all together as they all complement each other.

Training Yourself to Speed Read

Rather than spending a lot of money on expensive speed-reading courses, you may want to learn the skill yourself. You've already taken the first step by reading this book! After you've learned all of the methods along with some effective tips and tricks, you can actually train yourself to learn how to speed read. Here are some ways you can do this:

1. Train your eyes to minimize their movements

Before you learn how to speed read, you have to recognize and accept the fact that your eyes move A LOT when you're reading. For those who read normally, their eyes aren't able to move in a single, fluid motion. Instead, they keep fixating and backtracking on the words which they may have missed or those which they want to understand more. Once you start paying more attention to your eyes, you will be able to train them to minimize their movements.

Training your eyes doesn't always have to involve books. There are other ways to train your eyes, such as:

- Move your eyes from right to left while also moving your head from right to left.

- Move around while keeping your eyes steady. Even if you're moving your head, your eyes should always look forward.

- After you've practiced the first two methods, the next exercise is allowing your eyes to move with your head. In this case, keep your eyes centered, not looking to the right or to the left.

- The final exercise is to keep your head still while moving your eyes in a horizontal line from right to left and vice versa a couple of times.

These eye exercises allow you to maneuver your eyes comfortably as you need this skill when you're learning how to speed read.

2. During your training sessions, use a timer

A timer is a very important tool for speed reading. From the start, using a timer will allow you to know where you've started and will keep track of your progress each time you perform a self-check. There are different ways to use a timer. One way is to set a specific time then check how many pages you're able to read. Then after practicing with the speed-reading methods, test yourself again and see how much you have improved.

Another way you can use a timer is to read a couple of pages while you time yourself. Then, after your training sessions, read another set of pages which are roughly the same length as the first and check how long it takes you to get through these pages. If you want to keep track of your progress, keep a logbook or log sheet to record your progress. And each time you test yourself, try to beat your own record.

3. Set goals for yourself

It's always important to hold yourself accountable for the things you do. The same thing applies for when you're trying to learn something new. Set main goals as well as smaller goals which are more easily achievable. That way, each time you achieve these smaller goals, you will feel motivated to keep going. And the more small goals you complete, the closer you will get to achieving your main goals.

4. Read more books, articles, journals, and other types of reading materials

We go back to the old adage, "Practice makes perfect." This should be your motto when you're learning speed reading. No matter what new skill you're learning, practice is an essential part of the process. In this case, you can hone your speed-reading skills by reading more. Don't just stick with novels and articles you're interested in (although you may use these at the beginning to keep you motivated).

The better you get at speed reading, the more you should expand in terms of the types of material you're reading. That way, you will expose yourself to different subjects and different writing styles. Also, the more varied the materials you read are, the more you will learn how to control your reading pace. Then you will be able to determine when you need to slow down or speed up depending on what you're reading.

5. Test yourself regularly

Testing yourself regularly, or performing regular self-checks, is important for you to know which methods and techniques work for you. In order to see how much you've improved, know where you started and where you are at present. When testing yourself, use the same type and length of material. Don't use the same material repeatedly. For instance, you can find similar articles with similar lengths and use them for your self-checks. Then don't forget to keep a timer and a logbook on hand to ensure that your tests are accurately measured.

Helpful Speed-Reading Tips and Techniques

Reading is a basic skill. Those who love reading are constantly improving their memory, productivity, and even their health. But in our modern age where we are prone to getting an overload of information, we find ourselves struggling to finish everything we need to read each day. From reading articles, to reports, to emails, and more, there's so much to read and not enough time to do so! The number of things we have to read each day can make us feel tired or panicked. Soon, we see reading as a daunting task and not as something which will enrich our lives.

Of course, if you learn speed reading, you don't have to face this problem. Some people believe that speed reading is nothing but a myth. But the truth is just the opposite. Speed reading is a skill which you can learn and improve, as long as you keep practicing. Think of the speed-reading methods as a collection of conscious, mindful, and active strategies to employ to allow you to slow down or speed up your reading pace intentionally and as needed.

The methods we have discussed aren't the only ones which can help you become an effective speed reader. There are other reading strategies to learn which will allow you to double or even triple your reading speed while maintaining your reading comprehension. As you're learning how to speed read, keep these tips and techniques in mind as well:

- **Create an environment which is optimized for concentration**

This tip is especially beneficial for those who find it difficult to concentrate on what they're reading. Even before you start the learning process, it's important to create an optimal environment to set you up for success. This environment could be any room in your home or office that's completely free of distractions. Learning in such an environment will allow you to focus more on what you're reading and absorb the content more readily and quickly.

If you don't have access to such an environment, you may create your own "practice space." Simply position a table facing a wall and a chair in front of it. Then while you're practicing, wear a pair of noise-canceling headphones so you can read while listening to instrumental or classical music. This may help you concentrate more on what you're reading.

- **When reading online text or text on screens, use a variation of the hand pacing technique**

When you're reading text on your iPad or on a computer screen, you may increase your speed by using your finger to guide your eyes. You can also use other items such as a pen, a stylus or even a white index card while reading. This tip is especially useful if you're reading lengthy articles, emails, web pages, and PDFs. Reading text on a screen is much more tiring than reading printed, physical text. The good news is that you can also use speed-reading methods to increase your on-screen reading speed.

- **Avoid re-reading words**

This is one of the most common habits people have when reading. Going back to read the words you've already read slows your reading speed down significantly. If you observe how normal people read, you will see that their eyes jump and flit about. This is because they jump back to the words they've already read before they continue reading. These eye movements are counterproductive as your eyes should only flow smoothly back and forth when you're speed reading.

Most of the time, you don't even realize that you're doing this because this is the only way you know how to read. This makes it one of the more difficult habits to break, just like subvocalization. The best method to help minimize this habit is to use hand pacing. Also, the eye exercises we have used can help you learn how to control your eye movements better and more consciously.

- **Ask yourself questions about what you're reading**

This is another way for you to ensure that you're reading the material quickly and understanding it well, too. It's important to understand the structure and the framing of the text to process all of the details quickly. While you're reading the text, ask yourself some questions such as:

✓ What is this material all about?

✓ What is the main topic of this material?

✓ What is the central theme of this material?

✓ What information do I need to get from this material?

✓ Who wrote this material, and why is it relevant?

These types of questions help increase your reading speed because they decrease the amount of brain power you need to take in the meaning of the content. Also, asking yourself these questions will make you more aware of what you need to find out and why you're reading the text. In doing so, you become an active reader because you're invested in what you're reading.

- **When you're practicing, set a reading pace that's faster than your comprehension rate**

This tip is very useful when you're trying to practice the mechanical aspect of reading, which is the speed. Force yourself to read at a faster rate. Once you've gotten used to this pace, you will get a better idea of how to physically read faster. As you add the different speed-reading methods to your practice sessions, they will work together to increase your reading speed as well as your reading comprehension which, in turn, enhances your overall reading performance.

- **Turn the pages of the book faster**

Some say that this technique is quite trivial. But when you think about it, the concept behind it actually makes a lot of sense. On average, readers take about 4 seconds or so to turn the page of the book and continue what they're reading. This is the same amount of time proficient speed readers take to read the whole page! Slowly turning the page doesn't just slow down your reading speed, it might even affect your comprehension level. If it takes you as much as 4 seconds to just turn a page, this adds up to many minutes of time wasted when you read a whole book.

When you reach the end of a page, your thoughts don't end there. Ideally, you should read continuously so you don't break your concentration and thought process. But when your thought process gets cut at the end of the page and it takes you a significant time to turn to the next page and resume with your reading, it becomes challenging to comprehend what you're reading. There are even times when people forget the last part of what they were reading, and they have to go back! Now that's even more wasted time!

So, another technique is to practice turning the pages of books faster. That way, you will be able to maintain your reading speed, even as you go from one page of your book to another. This may take some practice, but it's an easy technique compared to the others we've discussed.

Chapter 13

Software Which Can Help
You Speed Read

Reading is one of the best and easiest ways to learn new things and new skills. Although you may be satisfied with how fast you're able to read right now, learning how to increase your reading speed will allow you to learn more things and to learn these things more effectively. And you can do this through speed reading.

We've already gone through the basic information about speed reading as well as the methods, tips, and techniques which can help you learn the skill. But in this modern, digital age, there a lot of helpful resources which you can learn online. Reading on computer screens and other types of screens are slightly different from reading on printed material. So, once you've learned how to speed read, you might also want to apply these techniques to when you're reading on your devices.

In this chapter, we'll learn more about how you can read digital text at an increased speed. Also, we'll go through some of the best speed-reading software which may help you in your quest to learn the skill of speed reading.

Speed Reading on the Computer Screen

Speed reading on a computer screen differs from speed reading on printed reading materials. This is because screens emit light, and you have to sit a certain way to read the text on a screen properly, unlike when you're reading books or other printed materials. To help you read faster on computer screens, here are some techniques:

- **If the text you're reading presents a challenge to your eyes, reformat the pages**

For instance, there are online pages which have fonts or font colors which are difficult to read, or which have too many images on them which make them look cluttered. In such instances, rather than skipping those pages, copy the text and paste in on a word processing software of your choice. After that, reformat the text to make it easier for you to read. You can change the font colors and sizes, giving them a more consistent appearance and size. You can also delete any images and adjust the spacing. After reformatting, you can either read the text on the screen or print it out and speed read as you would normally do.

- **Learn how to utilize various hardware and software features as pacers**

A pacer is a type of visual guide which you can use to guide your eyes down and across lines of text. This technique is similar to word pacing where you use your finger, a pen, or a card to guide your eyes.

This technique has a lot of benefits. For one, using a pacer forces your eyes to move at the same speed as the pacer and in the same direction. In other words, the pacer will improve your focus. When you use a pacer, it's virtually impossible to lose your place on the text. Also, it becomes easier to move forward as you're reading from one line to the next. Because of this, pacers will really help improve your reading speed.

One type of pacer that's available on your computer is a highlighter. Most word processing software has this feature and you can use it as your pacer. Just position your cursor at the beginning of the text then click on the highlighter. As you're reading, drag the cursor to the right end of each line and across the entire page to guide you. When you're done with a paragraph, simply release the mouse button to highlight the entire paragraph. Then repeat the process on the next paragraphs until you've finished the whole text.

This is a very effective method of using a pacer, but it can also be very troublesome, especially if you somehow use the backspace or delete key after you've highlighted the paragraph. So, if you're planning to use this method, make sure that you know how to undo the previous action so you don't end up deleting important information without meaning to.

Another pacer option available which is easier and safer to use is the cursor itself. Control the cursor using your mouse the same way you would control your finger using your hand. You can also use the scroll wheel of the mouse to move the document up and down as needed. Some people use the automatic scroll setting of their mouse. To do this, just set the speed of the mouse and allow it to go on an "auto-pilot" mode. Then sit back, relax, and read the text.

When you're reading printed materials, you can use index cards or other types of cards to cover the text above the line you're reading. Then, as you're reading, you move the card down to keep all of the text you've already read covered. This is one way to improve your reading speed while reading printed material. But you can also use this effective method on your computer screen.

All you have to do is scroll up the page until the line you're reading reaches the very top of your screen. Then, use your mouse to scroll down each time you finish a line of text, so you can move on to the next line. This way, you won't get confused while you're reading.

Another benefit of this technique is that the lines which you've already read won't be in your sights anymore. This prevents you from re-reading those words or lines, since doing this tends to slow you down.

Although reading on a computer screen slightly differs from reading on printed material, you can always find ways to apply the speed-reading methods we've discussed in the previous chapters here as well:

- For minimizing subvocalization, you can use the techniques such as chewing gum or listening to music while reading text on screens. These simple techniques work well whether you're reading printed material or text on your devices.

- For word chunking, you can also practice reading chunks of words on screens. However, you may want to shorten your training sessions when you're reading on screen because doing this causes more strain on your eyes than reading printed material.

- The same thing goes for when you're using your peripheral vision. You can use the techniques we have discussed and apply them to when you're reading text on the screen in order to expand your peripheral vision.

- Finally, for skimming and scanning, you can also use these methods for when you're reading on screen. In particular, using your mouse will prove to be very helpful for these methods.

Software which Can Help with Your Speed Reading

Anyone who learns about speed reading will definitely become interested in learning the skill. The good news about this skill is that you can teach yourself through different methods. We've talked about the basic methods to employ to learn speed reading, but did you know that there is a number of helpful software out there which can improve your learning journey? Although nothing really beats learning the "old-fashioned" way, using this software will allow you to keep up with the times while you're learning.

No matter what methods you plan to use, focus is key. You need to concentrate on the task in front of you if you want to learn how to become an effective speed reader. Let's take a look at some of the best software to use for your speed-reading learning journey:

1. AceReader Software

This is one of the most well-known and recognized speed-reading software which focuses on reading speed, comprehension, and reading fluency. It's very popular with reading education specialists, as it's meant to focus on issues such as processing, dyslexia, and vision training. According to StepWare Inc., the developer of the software, it's suitable for people of all professions, ages, and goals. There are several online editions of this software including Education, Family, and Personal. There's also the Classic edition which you can use offline.

Generally, those who use this software will take part in timed comprehension and reading activities. These will help increase reading speed with the help of pacing drills. The software also helps expand your peripheral vision through basic eye exercises and games. Use this software for 15 minutes at a time for about 2 or 3 times each week to see the first results. The learning outcomes you can expect to achieve include:

- Reduce the fixation time of the eyes;

- Expand the fixation zone of the eyes;

- Minimize subvocalization;

- Eliminate re-reading;

- Increase the speed of re-fixation.

This software also offers advanced tools for self-measurement and tracking. It includes hundreds of lessons for training, themed tests for reading comprehension, and a wide range of text materials of different levels for teachers and students.

2. RSVP Reader for Firefox

This software can help you double or even triple your reading speed. It comes with a plugin which allows you to read the text on the page by flashing word chunks in the toolbar. You have the option to choose the speed of the text and the number of words per chunk. It's the perfect tool for your training or practice sessions. If you want to push yourself, you can set a higher speed than what you're used to. This software is especially useful for training yourself to speed read on screen. It also serves as a pacer for when you're practicing.

3. Speed Reader-X

This software includes reading activities, tests, and lessons to help improve your reading speed. Although you need to pay for an annual subscription, it's one of the more affordable software options available. And the best part is that you can add an unlimited number of users to your account, making it a great choice for families.

When you start using this software, you would have to take a test to check your current reading speed. As you learn from the instruction provided by the software and perform the exercises, you need to take more tests to keep track of your speed-reading progress. The software includes exercises to train your eyes and expand your peripheral vision, two methods which can help you read faster.

The software also comes with a premium version which is preloaded with 17,000 eBooks for you to read and learn from. As you're practicing, you can modify the speed setting, adjust the text size, and change the fonts to make the text easier for you to read.

4. The 7-Speed-Reading Software

When it comes to speed reading, each person learns at a different rate, and this is because we all have different learning styles. The great thing about this particular software is that it offers 7 different learning strategies to help you become an efficient speed reader. With it, you can learn how to speed read in an interactive way, which is highly enjoyable. It also comes with different video lessons taught by some of the best speed-reading experts in the world.

This is a cloud-based software which consists of video training, software activities, social sharing, step-by-step modules, and advanced tracking options to monitor your progress. You may set-up 5 user accounts on this software along with an unlimited number of computer installs.

Since this software is cloud-based, you can access it from different devices. Whether you use a desktop, a tablet, a laptop or any other device, the program synchronizes the information automatically, allowing you to train no matter where you are. As long as you have a good internet connection and a device, you can use this software.

One excellent bonus feature of this software is that it comes with more than 20,000 eBooks for your training and practice sessions. Other features include posture training, personal goal setting, and more. It also comes with tools to help you train your brain, optic nerves, and eye muscles to improve your overall reading experience.

5. The Iris Reading Program

Finally, this is another one of the best software to use when you're learning speed reading. It offers a wide range of learning modules for you to choose, depending on your skill level and preferences. For those who are busy but would still like to learn speed reading, this software allows them to learn at their own pace and time on their devices. The step-by-step modules of this software include:

- Foundation

- Speed reading and proficiency

- Advanced memory and comprehension.

Although this software doesn't just focus on speed reading, it does offer a number of reading apps which will help you improve your reading performance. This makes it a comprehensive tool which even includes online classes.

Conclusion

Getting More Done Through Speed Reading

To reiterate, speed reading is a skill which allows you to read a printed or written material at a faster rate. You can achieve this by following the different methods we have learned about and through a lot of practice. With the right information and training, anyone can become an effective speed reader. The concept of speed reading was first taught by a woman named Evelyn Wood who was both a researcher and a school teacher. She taught the different methods of speed reading with the aim of teaching her students how to read at an increased speed while still understanding what they were reading.

Speed reading is a very important skill to learn, especially if your studies or work involve reading a lot of text each day. This skill allows you to cut down on your reading time without having to sacrifice your comprehension levels. As you learn the skill of speed reading, you'll realize that it involves some basic skills including:

- **Seeing:** This is the most crucial skill you need to have when you're speed reading. You need to see what you're reading and not just the words or phrases you're focusing on.

- **Reading:** Another big part of speed reading is reading itself. If you're not able to read well, it would be very difficult for you to learn the skill of speed reading. So, before you start learning how to speed read, you may have to practice reading first to get better at it.

- **Concentrating**: Speed reading requires concentration. This is why most of the speed-reading methods improve this skill as well. Speed reading is an active way of reading, and, without concentration, you won't be able to do it effectively.

Comprehending: For this skill, you will need a lot of practice to develop it. In fact, you may need as much practice as you need to learn the skill of speed reading. Without comprehension, your speed reading won't be very meaningful.

One of the main reasons why you might like to learn speed reading is that it allows you to read a lot more text which, in turn, allows you to get more things done. Learning this skill will allow you to read as fast as 600 words each minute or more depending on how much you practice and how fast you learn. Since speed reading also allows you to comprehend the material you've read fully, it's truly a very effective way of reading.

Speed reading saves you a lot of time, and the more you practice it, the better you get at it. This skill can help empower your personal and professional life. It also improves your ability to socialize with other people because you will be able to read up on the most current news and events with ease. With the knowledge you acquire from the articles, newspapers, and magazines you read, you will be able to contribute more to conversations.

Other great benefits of speed reading include improving your memory, boosting your confidence, adding to your knowledge bank, enhancing your problem-solving skills, and more. As you can see, this incredible skill will be beneficial in all aspects of your life. And, now that you know how to learn speed reading properly, you can start your learning journey. Good luck!